Exploring *Your* Horizons

CAREER AND PERSONAL PLANNING

D1317224

JUDI MISENER

Head of Program, Co-operative Education
Scarborough Centre for Alternative Studies
Scarborough, Ontario

Recognized by
The Conference Board of Canada

SUSAN BUTLER

Career Education Consultant
Toronto, Ontario

Consultants

David Chevreau
Magee Secondary School
Vancouver, British Columbia

Mary Chisholm
École Frank Ross Elementary School
Dawson Creek, British Columbia

Lina DiGregorio
Chestermear Middle School
Calgary, Alberta

Judy Griffiths
Highland Creek Public School
Uxbridge, Ontario

David Morris
Meadowbrook Middle School
Airdrie, Alberta

Joanne Twist
Peel Board of Education
Mississauga, Ontario

McGraw-Hill Ryerson Limited

Toronto   Montreal   New York   Auckland   Bogotá   Caracas
Lisbon   London   Madrid   Mexico   Milan   New Delhi
Paris   San Juan   Singapore   Sydney   Tokyo

McGraw-Hill
Ryerson Limited

*A Subsidiary of The **McGraw·Hill** Companies*

Exploring Your Horizons
Career and Personal Planning

ISBN 0-07-552864-9

http://www.mcgrawhill.ca

2 3 4 5 6 7 8 9 10 TRI 7 6 5 4 3 2 1 0 9

Printed and bound in Canada

Canadian Cataloguing in Publication Data

Misener, Judi, date
     Exploring your horizons: career and personal planning

Includes index.
ISBN 0–07–552864–9

1. Vocational guidance–Canada–Juvenile literature.
I. Butler, Susan (Dorothy Susan). II. Title.

HF5382.5.C2M57   1997   331.7'02   C97–930435–0

EDITORIAL DIRECTOR: Andrea Crozier
ASSOCIATE EDITOR: Jocelyn Wilson
SUPERVISING EDITOR: Nancy Christoffer
COPY EDITOR: Kathy Evans
PERMISSIONS EDITOR: Jacqueline Donovan
PRODUCTION CO-ORDINATOR: Yolanda Pigden
COVER AND INTERIOR DESIGN: Brant Cowie/ArtPlus Limited
ELECTRONIC PAGE MAKE-UP: Valerie Bateman/ArtPlus Limited
TECHNICAL ILLUSTRATIONS: Donna Guilfoyle/ArtPlus Limited
PART AND CHAPTER ILLUSTRATIONS: Chum McLeod
ADDITIONAL ILLUSTRATIONS: Harvey Chan, Laurel Dewan, Sami Suomalainen, Nicholas Vitacco
COVER IMAGE: Kennan Harvey/Tony Stone Images

Contents

Preface

••

Exploring Your Horizons will help you learn more about yourself, your future possibilities, and your community. How often have you been asked "What are you going to take in high school?" or "What do you want to do when you graduate?" Have you ever asked yourself "Who am I? What can I do? What is ahead of me? Where do I begin?" Exploring Your Horizons is designed to help you answer these questions and more. You will gain knowledge that will start you in the direction that best suits your talents, abilities, skills, and interests.

Before you can start planning your future education and career choices, you must first discover as much about yourself as possible. In **Part 1, Discovering Your Strengths,** you will gather information about yourself from a variety of sources. Once the information is collected, you will analyze it to see what it says about you. Then you will be able to set some short-term personal goals and longer-term education and career goals.

Knowing what choices are available is necessary before deciding which direction you will take. **Part 2, Discovering Pathways,** informs you of possibilities and enables you to research what might suit you best. You will learn more about education—high school, apprenticeships, college, and university, as well as other forms of learning available to you after you graduate. Your introduction to the workplace happens when you get your first paying job. You will learn how to earn and manage money. In the final chapter, you will examine the variety of employment opportunities available to you when you leave school. You can begin to match who you are with the type of job you would like to have.

Recognizing how you fit into your community is the first step to being a contributing member. In **Part 3, Setting Up Your Network,** you will meet people from your community and discover more about yourself by interacting with them. Discovering role models can help you determine what you want to be like when you are older. Connecting with mentors in your community will also help you get the support you might need.

Once you know what is available in your community and have learned more about the people who work there, your next step is to become actively involved. In **Part 4, Experiencing the Community as a Workplace,** you will examine what you learned from these experiences and how the skills you developed will assist you in the future.

In **Part 5, Establishing a Route,** you will compare school with the workplace to see how the skills and knowledge you develop in school are applied to real on-the-job situations. You will look closely at the skills you need for school and work success. Finally, you will learn how to prepare and present the portfolio materials you have gathered throughout the course for an evaluation conference.

Acknowledgements

My family gave me tremendous support as I spent hours on the computer and hours thinking about what this book should be like. I would like to give special thanks to my daughter, Meaghan, a student in grade eight. She was often my sounding board as well as a provider of some excellent ideas for activities and content.

Judi Misener

I would like to thank Peter, Ashley, and Lindsay for their encouragement and good humour throughout the length of this project

Susan Butler

Features

To make *Exploring Your Horizons* visually appealing to you, the material is presented in an easy-to-read format. Photographs, illustrations, charts, diagrams, and cartoons have been included.

What You Will Learn appears at the beginning of each chapter and is a brief summary of what is to come.

Terms to Remember are key words that appear in boldface and are defined when they first appear in the text. They are compiled and alphabetized in the glossary at the back of the book.

Activities such as surveying, interviewing, role-playing, researching, and reading provide opportunities for individual and group work in each chapter.

Journal writing allows you to reflect on, and gain further insight into, who you are.

Portfolio activities relate to personal interests, talents, education, possible careers, community involvement, and other areas. There is one or more in each chapter. You will collect these items in your Career Exploration Portfolio.

CHAPTER 11

Connecting in Your Community

What You Will Learn

- What job shadowing is and the procedures involved in it.
- What volunteer activities are available in your community and what skills you have as a potential volunteer.
- How to increase your involvement in the school community.
- How to create your own volunteer experience.

Terms to Remember

job shadowing
volunteer training programs
volunteer co-ordinators

114 SETTING UP YOUR NETWORK

Learning from Role Models

Many people attribute their success to a famous person they admired when they were young. That role model might have been a movie star, an inventor, a surgeon, or an athlete. They probably never spoke to that person, and yet he or she set a worthy example to follow.

People in the media also trigger the popularity of certain occupations. For example, there was an increase in the number of students who chose computer careers after the success of Bill Gates, who developed MS-DOS and founded Microsoft®. Every four years, the Olympics renews people's interest in sports careers. The "overnight successes" of performers like Alanis Morissette might spur individuals on to becoming singers. Because of the exposure, or extensive coverage, that people receive in the media, their actions have a strong impact on young people and the careers they choose for themselves.

Activity 3

Comparing Professionals

With a partner, pick a career that would be highly visible in the media; for example, politician, model, athlete, medical researcher, musician, or lawyer. Review back copies of newspapers and magazines at the library to find as many articles as you can on people in that profession. Identify the individuals who are receiving the most media attention. Record any personal attributes and actions that are mentioned in the articles. Then outline why that person would or would not make a good role model for young people. Report your findings to the class.

JOURNAL

Making Choices

In your journal, write an entry about education and career choices that you might make in the future and how they will affect your life as an adult.

PORTFOLIO

Visualizing What You Would Say

If you could spend ten minutes talking to a person you admire, what would you say? Would you explain why you admire him or her? Would you ask who he or she admired as a young person? Would you get an autograph? Would you ask about something specific he or she did? Write your reflections on a sheet of paper, or create a song about the experience, or draw a storyboard about the incident. File it in your portfolio.

Profiles of a famous Canadian or an interesting young person appear in most chapters. You can learn more about future possibilities for yourself through the lives of others. Questions relating to the content follow each profile.

In the News articles highlight people who have interesting accomplishments. They will provoke thought, discussion, and help you to set goals. At least one article appears in each chapter. It has relevant questions following it.

Case Studies appear periodically throughout the text and feature people whose life experiences offer good models from which to learn. The questions that follow each Case Study allow you to compare your own experiences with those of the people featured.

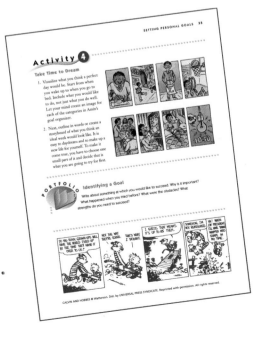

Cartoons selected for each chapter of this text will make you laugh and also learn! We believe that learning should always include humour.

 **Looking Back** sections at the end of every chapter feature questions that review and expand the chapter content.

 **Explorations** has activities that relate to the chapter content. They fall under the following headings:

Reflections offers an opportunity for journal writing, in which you record your feelings about an activity in the chapter.

Goals helps you set personal goals that relate to the chapter content.

Action! involves role-playing situations relevant to the chapter content.

In the **Featuring . . .** activities, you will be divided into groups to work on an edition of a magazine. For each chapter, your group will be assigned one of the following assignments.

Advice Column: Your team will create letters from readers asking for advice, and then write the answers.

Research: Using surveys, interviews, libraries, and the Internet, your team will research in greater depth a topic from the chapter, and then publish your findings.

Advertisement: Your team will create advertisements that relate to the content of the chapter. Be creative!

Editorial: Your team will write an editorial, which states an opinion and reasons for that opinion, on a given topic that relates to the chapter.

Personal Story/Interview: Your team will write a feature article on one person in the community whose story relates to the chapter.

Working through *Exploring Your Horizons*, your class will have created a number of editions of a magazine that cover all the topics. We recommend that a cover be designed and a unique name be given to your magazine.

Discovering Your Strengths

Attitudes

Friends

Helping Others

Jobs/Chores

Family/Culture

Health/Fitness

Awards/Special Accomplishments

Understanding yourself is the first step in educational and career planning. This understanding comes from collecting data, or information, about your likes and dislikes, your strengths and weaknesses. It comes from looking at past experiences. Your perception of self, or the way you see yourself, and the perception others have of you, assist you in answering the important question: "Who am I?" Once all the data is gathered, the second step is to examine it critically—what does it all mean? The final step is one of action—once you have a good understanding, what do you do with it? How can you make the most of your talents in the future?

Getting to Know Yourself

What You Will Learn

- How to collect and analyze data about yourself.
- Who you are in terms of values, attitudes, interests, aptitudes, and skills.
- How other people perceive who you are.
- How to identify your strengths and weaknesses.
- Which events in your life were important to you and helped shape who you are today.

Terms to Remember

profile	subjective
aptitudes	objective
skills	survey
values	questionnaire
attitudes	time line
journal	autobiography

Your interests, strengths, values, attitudes, and personal history all combine to make you who you are. In this chapter, you will gather and analyze information about yourself. You will look at how others see you to give you a more complete picture. Getting to know yourself is the first step on the path of determining what your future could be.

How You See Yourself

Filling in a chart is an organized way of developing your personal **profile**, or brief description of yourself. Following are two sample charts that will help you see how to explore your interests, aptitudes, skills, values, and attitudes. The charts do not describe a real person; they are samples only.

To begin, meet in small groups to discuss what you think the terms *interests*, *aptitudes*, *skills*, *values*, and *attitudes* mean. Have someone in the group record the ideas presented for each term. When you have reached a definition for each one, compare your ideas, as a class, to create final definitions. This will give you a clear idea of what you are describing when you fill in your own charts.

The first chart, Interests, Aptitudes, and Skills, is for recording activities and events in your life. **Aptitudes** refers to your natural talents and abilities, while **skills** means what you have learned to do well. Many of the categories in this chart relate to subjects studied in school. Remember that marks are important, but they are only one measurement. Your enjoyment and interest levels are important, too.

The second chart, Values and Attitudes, will help you explore your **values**, or what is important to you, and your **attitudes**, or how you view things.

FOR BETTER OR FOR WORSE © Lynn Johnston Prod., Inc. Reprinted with permission of UNIVERSAL PRESS SYNDICATE. All rights reserved.

Interests, Aptitudes, and Skills

CATEGORY	IN SCHOOL	OUT OF SCHOOL
Art	• it's okay • marks are average • like doing perspective	• design t-shirts • make posters • like doodling
Music	• like playing the flute • learning to read music is interesting • performing is exciting	• listen to it all the time • go to concerts • buy CDs of my favourite musicians
Sports	• like phys. ed. • am on intramural teams • swim a lot	• am on a hockey team • play baseball
Technology	• use the computer as much as I can • use the Internet • like making things out of wood	• program the VCR • use the computer • fix bicycles
Math	• have good marks in math • like the challenge • like applying it to real situations	• have a bank account • make change • take measurements for building things
Science	• like the experiments • understand it easily • like the pictures in science books	• watch science shows on TV • use a telescope • have an aquarium
Language Arts	• have difficulty with spelling • love to read • like to give presentations	• take acting classes • keep a daily journal • go to the library every week
Media	• like it when we have videos in class • enjoy making videos • enjoy reading newspapers	• watch TV • go to movies • keep photo albums
Social Studies	• interesting • like videos about other places • like drawing maps	• like to travel • collect souvenirs • read history books
Jobs/Chores	• sell tickets • am on a stage crew • am a recycling monitor	• baby-sit • deliver newspapers • clean my room
Awards/Special Accomplishments	• earned five certificates last year	• hockey team finished first in league

Values and Attitudes

CATEGORY	ACTIVITIES	BELIEFS
Friends	• group work is fun • talk a lot in class • talk on the phone	Friends should be: • honest • supportive • dependable • fun
Helping Others	• read to younger kids • help kids with special needs • take part in 4H Club community projects	• helping younger kids makes me feel good about myself • homeless people need our help • working at the food bank is important
Family/Culture	• eat together • keep up my cultural traditions	• my family means a lot to me • eating together keeps the family together • family traditions are important
Health/Fitness	• am very active • like being outside • love food	• eating good food is healthy • playing sports is good exercise • staying at home when you're sick stops germs from spreading
Attitudes	• work hard in school • am friendly • am optimistic	• doing well in school is important • helping others is good • being positive makes everything easier

Activity 1

Creating Your Personal Charts

Create an Interests, Aptitudes, and Skills chart like the one on page 4. On sheets of paper, make three columns with the headings *Category*, *In School*, and *Out of School*. Then write your subject names down the left side of the page under the heading *Category*. Beside each subject, give brief examples of your interests, aptitudes, and skills in that subject, both in and out of school. Refer to the sample to help you get started.

Then create a Values and Attitudes chart like the one on this page, with three columns titled *Category*, *Activities*, and *Beliefs*. Write the category headings down the left side of the page. Fill in your chart, giving examples of activities and what you think of them, for each category.

Change or add to the categories in your charts, if necessary. Try to write at least three points for each category. Be honest and thorough. Use descriptive words. Describe what you are proud of, what you like, and what you do not like. Examine both what you do and what you *think* about what you do.

These charts will tell you a lot about yourself when you analyze them. You will learn what your strongest interests are, where your talents lie, and what your values and attitudes are. These facts will be very important to you when you develop your interests, skills, and social abilities in school, in the community, and, eventually, in your career.

1. Study your charts. Circle the categories that contain the most positive statements. Then choose either question 2 or 3 to complete.

2. Using your charts as a guide, write several paragraphs about yourself.

3. Write a poem or song about yourself, or draw a picture, describing what qualities or interests make you unique.

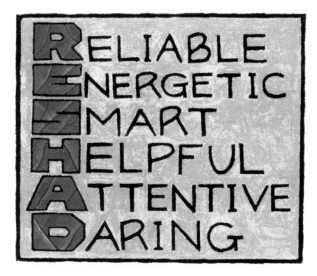

4. As a class, make lists of the qualities you expect from your friends, your teachers, and your parents. Underline the common items in the lists. How would you rate yourself for each quality? For example, if honesty is on your list, think about how honest *you* are. Are you always, sometimes, or never honest? Then create a list of the characteristics that describe you best.

 File your charts, paragraphs, poem, song, or drawing, and list in your portfolio.

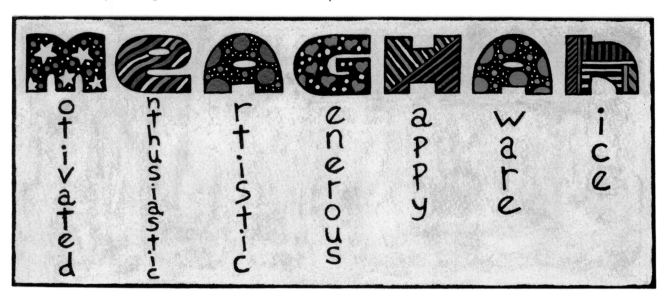

Activity 2

Determining What You Value

From a cross-Canada study of people's values, a list of values important to teenagers was developed. These values are: friendship, freedom, privacy, being popular, recognition, excitement, being loved, success, a comfortable life, and family life.

On a sheet of paper, write these values in their order of importance to you. Then compare your list with the chart at right.

Teenagers' Values Across Canada

VALUE	PERCENT VIEWING AS "VERY IMPORTANT"
Friendship	91
Being Loved	87
Freedom	84
Success	78
A Comfortable Life	75
Privacy	68
Family Life	65
Excitement	58
Recognition	41
Being Popular	21

Activity 3

Identifying Family Influences

List ways your family has influenced your values and behaviour. Consider the rules you were taught at home, what things your family considers to be important, and the routines and daily habits, likes and dislikes, that come from your parents or guardians.

PORTFOLIO

Creating a Collage

Using photographs, drawings, objects, or pictures from magazines, create a collage that reflects who you are. Study your collage and think about yourself. Create a slogan, phrase, or title that describes you, and add it to your collage.

Recording Your Day

A **journal** is a record of events in a person's life and his or her thoughts and feelings about these events. A journal can be kept daily, weekly, or only occasionally. Each entry is dated so that, in the future, the person will know when the events took place. It is usually written in the past tense. Some people draw in their journals or include mementos, like ticket stubs to a special event. A journal can be a notebook, a diary, a computer file—anything you want to use that works for you. Read the sample journal entry at right.

Keep a journal for two weeks. At the end of each day, write about what you did and how you felt. Compare the ideas in your journal with those in your charts. Add to the charts if you learned more about yourself by keeping this journal.

> SEPTEMBER 2, 19__
>
> Today was my first day at a new school. I was excited, but really nervous, too. I felt better when I saw that I knew a few people in each class. I think I will like most of my teachers; that is, if I can find their classrooms! The school is so big, and having to find my way around is so confusing. I guess I'll get to know the school sooner or later. I met a few kids that I'd like to make friends with. I'll see what happens.

How Others See You

How you see yourself and how others perceive you are sometimes quite different. Your view of yourself is **subjective**. Your past experiences, your place in the family, your emotions, interests—many things influence how you see yourself. The way other people see you is **objective**. They are detached, or at least removed, from that first-hand knowledge. This enables them to see you as you are at that moment. They can observe your strong and your weak points. They might notice qualities about you that you were not aware of. They might see abilities that you do not even notice because you have had them for so long or because you do not see them as being unique. What they see might boost your self-confidence, surprise you, or, at least, be of interest to you. Learning how others see you can further develop your personal profile.

Activity 4

Taking a Survey

To obtain an objective viewpoint about something or someone, a **survey** is a useful tool. A number of people are asked the same set of questions. Their answers are compiled and the results are analyzed, either to get specific information or a general picture of a topic.

You will be taking a survey about yourself.

1. Create a **questionnaire** that asks direct and personal questions about how people see you. Study the following example to give you an idea of how it could look.

Sample Questionnaire

As part of a school assignment, I would like to know how you see me. Your opinions will be helpful as I learn more about myself. Please take the time to answer these questions.

1. My best qualities are. . .

2. In what area could I improve?

3. Give five words that describe me.

Thank you.

2. Select a close friend, a family member, a teacher, and one other person whom you trust. They will answer the questions about you.

3. To conduct your survey, ask each of the people the questions yourself and write down the answers, or hand out copies of your questionnaire for them to fill out. Use the following format to compile their answers. Record their names and the answers to each question beside the question number.

Survey Results

	(Friend)	(Family Member)	(Teacher)	(Other Person)
1. My best qualities are:				
2. Area in which I could improve:				
3. Five words that describe me:				

4. After you have compiled your survey results, write down something from the survey that surprised you, something that pleased you, and something that you will try to improve.

Add any new information to the paragraphs you wrote about yourself earlier.

Attach the survey results to your paragraphs and file them in your portfolio.

Your Past Experiences

Looking back at previous experiences in your life provides other important puzzle pieces for understanding who you are. You can learn from your past triumphs and disappointments. Understanding the past and the present help you to plan your future.

PROFILE

Jim Carrey—Alllrrighty Then

Born on January 17, 1962, in Newmarket, Ontario, Jim Carrey was the youngest of four children. Throughout his childhood, his father, Percy, suffered from manic depression and his mother, Kathleen, had kidney problems. The family's financial situation was like a roller coaster ride, going from middle-class comfort to poverty. Jim was put down by his peers because of his family circumstances. To overcome this, he developed funny routines to make them laugh so he would be accepted.

When Jim was 16 and in his first year of high school, his father lost his job as an accountant and could not find other work. The family became homeless, and Jim was forced to drop out of school to help earn money. After working as an office building cleaner with his family, he decided he had to do what he loved and had a talent for—comedy. Five years and several movies later, he became a successful stand-up comic.

In 1990, his character Fire Marshal Bill became a hit on the television series *In Living Colour*. Then he was in *Doing Time on Maple Drive*, a made-for-TV movie, which was nominated for an Emmy award. Unfortunately, before he became a big success, his mother died of kidney failure. He also ended his seven-year marriage to Melissa Womer, with whom he had a daughter, Jane, now eight.

In 1994, Jim Carrey had three movies playing at the theatres—*Ace Ventura: Pet Detective; The Mask;* and *Dumb and Dumber*—all of which became blockbusters! Unfortunately, with his success came tragedy. His father, with whom Jim was close, died unexpectedly.

Since then, Jim has appeared in *Batman Forever; Ace Ventura: When Nature Calls; The Cable Guy;* and *Liar, Liar.* He received $20 million for the last film, the highest amount ever given to a comedian in a film. He has also been both host and guest on many talk shows. Besides having won numerous awards, Jim Carrey is immortalized on the Hollywood Walk of Fame.

1. Write about what reading this profile makes you realize about people.

2. Using information from the profile, create a time line like the following, recording the important dates and events in Jim Carrey's life.

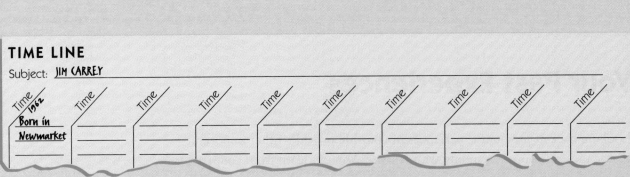

TIME LINE
Subject: JIM CARREY

Time 1962 Born in Newmarket

Time

Time

Time

Time

Time

Time

Time

Time

Time

Activity 5

Creating a Personal Time Line

Think about the major events in your life that changed both your life and you. If you consider these events for a while, you might start remembering things that you have not thought about for a long time. Now, draw a **time line** on a sheet of paper. List the important dates and events in the order they happened. When you have finished, share your time line with classmates, friends, and family members to see if they can add anything to it. Do you feel like you know yourself better now?

 You might wish to add your time line to your portfolio.

Activity 6

Representing Your Life

Write an **autobiography** or a song or draw a storyboard about your life. Include factual details, such as where you were born, where you have lived, who is in your family, and so on. Include three major events that had a big influence on you. Some examples are the birth of a sibling, a major accomplishment, the purchase of a pet, or something unfortunate, such as the death of a grandparent, or a family separation.

 You might wish to share your work with a teacher, parent/guardian, or friend and add it to your portfolio.

Activity 7

Creating a Box of Treasures

Create a box of treasures from your personal belongings. Include such things as a photograph of your favourite person, something you made, or something related to a hobby. Whatever you include should represent who you are. Put the box in a safe place. You might want to add new items to it periodically to update any changes in your life or create a new box to have different "time capsules" of yourself.

Activity 8

Assessing Your Past

Review your time line or autobiography, and then answer the following questions on a sheet of paper or in your journal.

1. What is your best memory? Why?

2. How have your past experiences affected who you are today?

3. Add any data from your past to the paragraphs you have already written about yourself.

IN THE NEWS

A Budding Author

by Robin Harvey

Writer Lisa Pileggi says inspiration can hit her anytime, day or night.

Lisa, a public school student who has written stories "ever since kindergarten," keeps a tape recorder near her bed to take down any thoughts that she doesn't want to lose. The 12-year-old Toronto girl is the only Canadian featured in a new collection of short stories written by young people around the world and published by Populace Press.

Lisa says she gets two types of inspiration for her work. One is when an idea, like the story her grandmother once told her about seeing a vision as a young woman in Italy, "lights a spark and I just get thinking and thinking and I have to write it down. Other times I get a block so I just write down ideas like 'what if a train crashed, what if a boy saw it, and . . .' Then I join them and jumble them and something comes out of it and becomes a story."

But Lisa considers herself to be an "ordinary kid." These days most of the Grade 7 student's time is taken up with homework. "I'm in extended French and we really have a lot of work, so I haven't had a lot of time to think about being published," she says. "But it's nice seeing the book there in the bookstore and knowing I'm one of the

Writer Lisa Pileggi displays the book *Imagine*, in which two of her stories appear.

authors people can buy." She's the only writer to have two short stories featured in the anthology called *Imagine*.

Lisa was surfing the Internet last year and found a Web site where young authors could submit stories for others' reading pleasure. She sent several in. Later a British publisher contacted her by e-mail and asked if she'd send in some new, never-published material for their planned collection. It took her about a week each to write, polish, and perfect the two stories. Even so, she says she was "amazed" when they were selected. "I didn't know if anything would come of it, so it was pretty amazing," she says. "I always dreamed of this."

When she was younger, Lisa wrote about animals, including a group of mice with human traits

and problems. She had been heavily involved in reading R.L. Stine, the popular author of *Goosebumps*, when she created the stories for *Imagine*. Lately she's started enjoying science-fiction.

Lisa also plays the piano and flute, and loves doing jigsaw puzzles. She also is concerned about the environment. "I'd love to be able to go down to the beach and swim or go to High Park and swim but that's impossible now. Maybe we can do something to make a difference and it won't always be that way."

1. Name the events that led to Lisa's success.

2. Discuss what this article tells you about young people.

Looking Back

1. How is knowing yourself helpful for your education and future career?

2. What is the benefit of knowing how others see you?

3. Why is being aware of your weaknesses as well as your strengths helpful?

EXPLORATIONS

Reflections

You have the opportunity to participate in an exchange program to another province. You will spend time with a student and his or her family in their home and the student will come to your home. It is important that a good match is made between you and the exchange student. You are, therefore, required to submit a description of yourself. Begin with the sentence "I am a person who . . ."

Action!

In groups, brainstorm a list of skills. Each member selects one skill at which he or she is competent. Imagine that you are together in a foreign city and have become lost. Develop a script about how you would combine your skills to find your way. Then role-play the scenario. Think of another problem that needs to be solved and role-play the outcome.

Featuring. . .

Advice Column: What advice would you give to teens who feel they do not fit in?

Research: Conduct a survey of teenagers' values using those listed in the Teenagers' Values Across Canada chart on page 7. Select whom you want to survey. For example, you might want to survey students and teachers and compare their responses. Compare the responses you get with the percentages in the chart.

Editorial: Write an editorial on the topic "Following the Crowd."

Personal Story/Interview: A mix of many cultures adds an interesting dimension to every classroom, school, and community. The differences in cultures are fascinating. Write a story about someone in your class, school, or community who is from a culture different from your own.

Advertisement: For the same exchange trip as mentioned in Reflections, you need to describe what you would like your exchange partner to be like. State your requirements in a "Wanted" poster or as an advertisement.

Intelligences, Personality Types, and Learning Styles

What You Will Learn

- About the variety of intelligences and which ones apply to you.
- What an emotional quotient is and how it contributes to your life skills.
- About personality types and how to analyze your own and others.
- About different learning styles, how to identify which one you have and know how it can improve your learning.
- Whether you work best on your own or with a group of people.
- What left-brained and right-brained means, and how the terms apply to how you think and act.

Terms to Remember

psychology

intelligence quotient

literacy

numeracy

multiple intelligences

emotional quotient

personality type

auditory learners

visual learners

kinaesthetic learners

right-brained

left-brained

I n this chapter, you will continue to learn more about yourself by using methods that have been designed by specialists in the field of **psychology**. Psychology is the study of human nature. There are many theories, based on years of research, on how and why we behave the way we do. Some are featured in this chapter. You will discover many different ways to figure out who you are. When you know yourself, you can make choices and decisions that are right for you. You can make plans that fit who you are. You will also be able to compare yourself to others, and discover what characteristics you have in common and what your differences are.

Seven Ways to Be Smart

Have you heard of the term IQ? It is the short form for **intelligence quotient**. The quotient is a number that is determined from the results of a written test. The test focusses on ability in **literacy** (language) and **numeracy** (numbers). The higher the number, the greater the potential intelligence. The IQ test has been a standard for determining intelligence for decades. Average intelligence is a score of 100. But is it the only way to measure intelligence?

Psychologist Dr. Howard Gardner believes that the IQ test is too limiting and that humans are intelligent in many areas. After extensive research, he has identified seven kinds of intelligence, or **multiple intelligences**. Psychologist Dr. Thomas Armstrong uses the phrase "Seven Kinds of Smarts." Another way of thinking about how people are "smart" is to think about the many ways that people are talented.

Music Smart (Musical Intelligence)

This intelligence is based on how musical you are. People who respond to rhythm and beat, who perform either vocally or with an instrument, or who compose music have this kind of "smart."

Activity ①

Music-Smart Quiz

On a sheet of paper, write down the activity title and the statements that apply to you.

1. I have a pleasant singing voice.

2. I can tell when a musical note is off-key.

3. I frequently listen to music on the radio, cassettes, or CDs.

4. I play a musical instrument.

5. I often walk around with a song running through my mind.

6. I can easily keep time to a piece of music.

7. I know the tunes to many songs.

8. I often make tapping sounds or hum while studying or learning something new.

Body Smart (Bodily-Kinesthetic Intelligence)

This intelligence relates to physical movement. Each person possesses a certain control over body movements, balance, agility, and grace.

Activity ❷ •

Body-Smart Quiz

On a sheet of paper, write down the activity title and the statements that apply to you.

1. I participate in at least one sport or physical activity on a regular basis.

2. I find it difficult to sit still for long periods of time.

3. I like working with my hands by doing activities such as sewing, carving, model building.

4. I frequently use hand gestures or other forms of bodily language when I am talking.

5. I need to touch things in order to learn more about them.

6. I enjoy daredevil amusement rides or similar thrilling physical experiences.

7. I think I am well co-ordinated.

8. I need to practise a new skill rather than read about it or watch a video describing it.

People Smart (Interpersonal Intelligence)

This intelligence is about person-to-person relationships. It is the ability to interact with others, understand them, and interpret their behaviour. It is how you notice contrasts in moods, and sense what people are thinking or feeling without them telling you.

Activity ❸ •

People-Smart Quiz

On a sheet of paper, write down the activity title and the statements that apply to you.

1. My friends come to me for advice.

2. I prefer team sports, such as basketball, instead of solo sports, such as diving.

3. When I have a problem, I usually talk to another person about it instead of working it out on my own.

4. I have three close friends.

5. I would rather play games like Monopoly with other people instead of watching television or playing computer games by myself.

6. I am comfortable in a crowd of people.

7. I am involved in extra-curricular activities at school or in my community.

8. I would rather spend time with my friends than stay at home.

Self Smart (Intrapersonal Intelligence)

This intelligence relates to how well you understand yourself. It is the ability to have insight into who you are, what you feel, and why you are the way you are. A strong intrapersonal intelligence can lead to high self-esteem and a strength of character that can be used to solve personal problems.

Activity 4 ···

Self-Smart Quiz

On a sheet of paper, write down the activity title and the statements that apply to you.

1. I like to spend time alone thinking and reflecting about my life.

2. I like to take quizzes that enable me to learn more about myself.

3. If I have a personal problem, I do not let it get me down. I solve it and get going.

4. I have goals for my life that I think about regularly.

5. I consider myself to be very independent.

6. I keep a personal diary or journal to record my thoughts about what happens to me.

7. I often prefer to be alone than with a large group of people.

8. I have a very clear idea of my strengths and weaknesses.

Picture Smart (Visual-Spatial Intelligence)

This intelligence, which relies on the sense of sight and the ability to visualize an object, includes the ability to create pictures in your head.

Activity 5 ···············

Picture-Smart Quiz

On a sheet of paper, write down the activity title and the statements that apply to you.

1. I often see clear images when I close my eyes.

2. I am good at co-ordinating colours.

3. I frequently use a camera or a video camera to record what I see around me.

4. I enjoy doing jigsaw puzzles, 3-D puzzles, and mazes.

5. I can generally find my way around unfamiliar territory.

6. I like to draw or doodle.

7. I can look at an object one way and imagine what it would look like from a different angle.

8. I prefer reading articles and books that have lots of diagrams and pictures.

Word Smart (Linguistic Intelligence)

This kind of intelligence relates to words and language, both written and spoken. People who are highly skilled writers, who have large vocabularies, and who speak many languages have this kind of intelligence.

Activity 6

Word-Smart Quiz

On a sheet of paper, write down the activity title and the statements that apply to you.

1. Books are very important to me.

2. I can hear words in my head before I read, speak, or write them down.

3. I get more out of listening to the radio than I do from watching television or videos.

4. I enjoy playing games that involve words.

5. I enjoy entertaining myself or others with tongue twisters or puns.

6. Other students sometimes stop and ask me to explain the meaning of a word I am using.

7. Language Arts, French, and history are easier for me than math and science.

8. I often write stories or poems in my spare time.

Logic Smart (Logical-Mathematical Intelligence)

This intelligence is the ability to solve logical problems and equations mentally. A person with this intelligence is good with numbers and doing calculations.

Activity 7

Logic-Smart Quiz

On a sheet of paper, write down the activity title and the statements that apply to you.

1. I can easily compute numbers in my head.

2. Math and science are among my favourite subjects in school.

3. I enjoy playing games or solving brain teasers that require logical thinking.

4. I am interested in new developments in science.

5. I am good with computers and enjoy working on them.

6. I like to do experiments and figure out how things work.

7. I can easily see numerical patterns.

8. I like to put things in order.

PROFILE

World of Opportunities Await Bailey

by Randy Starkman

As a kid, Bailey always dreamed of soaring through the air, but even he never expected to reach such heights. He owns the 100-metre world track title, Olympic gold medal and world record, plus another Olympic Gold from anchoring Canada's 4 x 100-metre relay team's stirring win over the U.S.

"I never saw myself doing this at this level," he said. "I never dreamed it would be a worldwide thing. My brother and I were well-known athletes in Oakville, but I didn't think I'd be a household name worldwide. That's big. It doesn't get any bigger than that, I guess."

But even as he gets caught up in the whirlwind that comes with fame, Bailey has a firm grasp on where he's heading. His aspirations can't be confined to a track and field stadium. He was a serious businessperson before he was a serious sprinter. "I'm looking for new challenges other than track," Bailey says. "Track and field is definitely my tool to get where I want to go, to the successful podium. It's so wide-open right now. That's what I love the most."

Coming soon to a convention hall near you: Donovan Bailey, motivational speaker. Bailey is determined to improve himself in the area of public speaking. "I think it's one of my weaknesses, getting up and presenting my story and doing it fluently," Bailey said. "If it's one of my weaknesses, it can only be an asset if I continue to correct myself just as I do in track, so I can get to the point where I'm comfortable."

What has made Bailey so marketable besides the titles he's gained is that he's eloquent, forthright, and has the smile and charm sought by advertisers. He's impressed observers with his willingness to tackle tough issues head-on.

"One thing about Donovan is he's incredibly honest," says his coach, Dan Pfaff. "He'll look you in the eyes and tell you what's going on. The eyes generally don't lie and I think people recognize this instantly."

Bailey was on Wall Street on behalf of Bell Mobility when the company's stock went public. It gave him the chance to meet with some big financiers. "When I go out, the job I do can open doors for younger guys." It also enables Bailey to open the door toward his biggest goal—making a smooth transition from the track to the boardroom.

So the next step for Donovan Bailey is the motivational circuit. But what is left to motivate him? He speaks of running "the perfect race," but what appears to excite him most is a team goal—chasing the world record in the relay. With relay mainstays Glenroy Gilbert and Bruny Surin, whom he regards as good friends, he wants to keep beating the Americans and take their world record, too.

Bailey would like to lower the Canadian record of 20.17 seconds, set in 1991 by Atlee Mahorn, to a more respectable world level.

When asked what message he had for high school students, Donovan Bailey said, "Just pursue your dreams. Stay strong. You can do it. Whatever it is you want to do, just work at it. Stay positive."

Reprinted with permission—The Toronto Star Syndicate.

1. Identify the types of intelligences you think Donovan Bailey has.

2. List the careers Donovan has and will be involved in.

Activity 8

Identifying Your Strongest Intelligence

For each quiz you just completed, add up the number of statements you wrote. Each quiz has a possibility of eight. In which quiz did you have the most answers? The least? Which kind of "smarts" do you have? You probably had some answers in each quiz; you probably have more than one kind of intelligence, with some ability in all of them.

Each individual is born with a unique combination of talents. Most researchers believe there are more than those listed earlier in the chapter. The next two qualities are also considered to be forms of intelligence.

Humour Intelligence

Having a highly developed sense of humour and the ability to create humour is considered to be a form of intelligence. Writers, cartoonists, and comedians are in this category. How is your sense of homour?

Emotional Intelligence

According to a leading expert, Dr. Goleman, your **emotional quotient** (EQ) is your ability to handle your emotions. It refers to how you cope with demands and expectations, how you adapt to meet challenges. Dr. Goleman believes it is the most important form of intelligence. It includes your ability to manage your time and to finish what you start. Your EQ determines how successful and happy you will be and how long you will live. We can think of EQ in this way: Being smart does not matter if you do not know what to do with it!

Activity 9

Identifying a Person's Intelligence

On a sheet of paper, write the name of a person you know personally beside each question number. If you cannot think of someone who is right for the question, then give the name of a famous person.

1. If I ever get lost, I hope I am with —.

2. If I ever own a basketball team, I want — to be a player.

3. If I move to a new place and need to learn my way around, I hope I can be with —.

4. If we enter a poster contest, I want — on my team.

5. When my radio breaks, I hope — will be home so I can call for help.

6. If I work on an invention, I want — to help me.

7. I definitely want to have — on my debating team.

8. If I start a musical group, I sure hope I can get — to join.

9. For a fun time at my party, I will invite —.

10. When I need advice about a problem, I will always call on —.

11. We are going to try to get the school cafeteria to change its menu. I hope — will be our leader when we do this.

12. We are moving to a new community and I have to start at a new school. I hope — will stay in touch and help me adjust.

Personality Type

Determining your **personality type** can help you decide on the kind of career you might want. Just as experts have studied human intelligence, they have also studied human personality. There are numerous personality tests that can be taken. The results are scored and a person's personality type is defined. One of the most famous of these tests is called the Myers-Briggs Type Inventory, after the mother-and-daughter team that invented it. Their findings have been the basis of other forms of personality tests. A very popular and fun one to do is called True Colours.

Four colours—orange, blue, green, and gold—are used to represent the four different parts of your personality. Each personality part is represented by a different colour and refers to different personality characteristics. Just as some of you prefer to write with your right or left hand, you also have a preferred part of your personality that you like to use the most. Although you really have all four colours or parts in your personality, everyone has a favourite personality colour that is naturally like him or her. The colour that describes you the best is your dominant or strongest colour. Read the following descriptions. On a sheet of paper, write the names of the colours in the order *most like you* to *least like you*. Remember, all the personality colours are positive, and everyone has some of each of the personality colours.

Curious Green
Basic need is for mental power, or to be seen as smart.

Characteristics
- Analytical and conceptual (examines things carefully, thinks in terms of ideas or concepts)
- Independent, self-motivated, and logical
- Thinks a lot
- Values gaining and sharing knowledge

Strengths and Needs
- Possesses problem-solving skills
- Sees relationship of parts to whole
- Requires independence of thought and opportunity to work alone
- Needs to ask questions to satisfy curiosity

Adventurous Orange

Basic needs are for action, excitement, freedom, and to act on impulse.

Characteristics
- Playful and fun-loving
- Competitive and adventurous
- Likes to take risks

Strengths and Needs
- Exhibits high energy and zeal
- Seizes opportunities; is clever
- Needs hands-on approach
- Requires variety and flexibility
- Possesses a sense of humour

Responsible Gold

Basic needs are for structure, security, and to be of help to others.

Characteristics
- Organized and plans ahead
- Dependable, loyal, and responsible
- Follows the rules

Strengths and Needs
- Respects authority
- Needs order and sequence
- Responds well to a structured, stable environment

Harmonious Blue

Basic needs are for harmony and positive, close relationships.

Characteristics
- Friendly and sensitive
- Imaginative and communicative
- Wants to make the world a better place

Strengths and Needs
- Values the feelings of others
- Creates harmony
- Sees various sides of an issue
- Needs to feel emotionally connected with others
- Desires affirmation and encouragement from others

Activity 10

Determining Your Colour

From the previous descriptions, determine which colour is most like you. If you have difficulty deciding between two colours, ask a friend, a teacher, or a parent/guardian for his or her opinion. On a sheet of paper, write your colour as a heading, and list the characteristics, strengths, and needs for that colour. You might wish to file the description in your portfolio.

Activity 11

Discovering Your Colour Mates

Have each corner of the classroom represent one of the four colours. Go to the corner that represents your colour. Are you surprised by who is with you? With your group, discuss your colour's personality traits and give examples of how you have those traits. What are your values? What careers do you think suit your colour's characteristics?

Learning Styles

To learn, we depend on our senses to bring information to our brain. Most people tend to use one of their senses more than the others. Some people learn best by listening. They are called **auditory learners**. Other people learn best by reading or seeing pictures. They are **visual learners**. Still others learn best by touching and doing things. They are called **kinaesthetic learners**.

Scientists and psychologists do not know why people use one sense more than the others. Maybe the sense we use the most just works better for us. Knowing your learning style might help you learn better and more efficiently. It might also explain why some things are more difficult for you to learn.

It is not unusual to use different learning styles for different tasks. For instance, you might repeat your German lessons out loud to prepare for a test, but study your textbook to prepare for your math quiz. You might repeat some experiments you did in class to prepare for your science test. In these cases, you are using an auditory style to learn a language, a visual style to learn math, and a kinaesthetic style to learn science. Each one helps you learn what you need to know.

Another component of learning styles is whether you like to work in groups or by yourself.

Activity 12

Identifying Your Learning Style

For these questions, choose the first answer that comes to your mind. Do not spend too much time thinking about any question. Record your answers on a sheet of paper by listing the number of the question and the letter of your answer.

1. Which way would you rather learn how a computer works?
   a. watching a video about it
   b. listening to someone explain it
   c. taking the computer apart and trying to figure it out for yourself

2. When you are not sure how to spell a word, which of these are you most likely to do?
   a. write it out to see if it looks right
   b. sound it out
   c. write it out to sense how it feels

3. If you were at a party, what would you be most likely to remember the next day?
   a. the faces of the people there, but not the names
   b. the names but not the faces
   c. the things you did and said while you were there

4. How would you rather study for a test?
   a. read notes, read headings in a book, look at diagrams and illustrations
   b. have someone ask you questions, or repeat facts silently to yourself
   c. write notes out on index cards and make models or diagrams

5. What do you find most distracting when you are trying to concentrate?
   a. visual distractions
   b. noises
   c. other sensations like hunger, tight shoes, or worry

6. How do you prefer to solve a problem?
   a. make a list, organize the steps, and check them off as they are done
   b. make a few phone calls and talk to friends or experts
   c. make a model of the problem or walk through the steps in your mind

7. Which are you most likely to do while standing in a long line at the movies?
   a. look at the posters advertising other movies
   b. talk to the person next to you
   c. tap your foot or move around in some other way

8. You have just entered a science museum. What will you do first?
   a. find a map showing the locations of the various exhibits
   b. talk to a museum guide and ask about exhibits
   c. go into the first exhibit that looks interesting and read directions later

9. When you are happy, what are you most likely to do?
   a. grin
   b. shout with joy
   c. jump for joy

10. Which would you rather go to?
    a. an art class
    b. a music class
    c. an exercise class

11. Which of these do you do when you listen to music?
    a. daydream (see images that go with the music)
    b. hum along
    c. move with the music, tap your foot, etc.

12. How would you rather tell a story?
    a. write it
    b. tell it out loud
    c. act it out

13. Which kind of restaurant would you rather not go to?
    a. one with the lights too bright
    b. one with the music too loud
    c. one with uncomfortable chairs

   Total your a's, b's, and c's.
   - *If you scored mostly a's*, you have a visual learning style. You learn by seeing and looking.
   - *If you scored mostly b's*, you have an auditory learning style. You learn by hearing and listening.
   - *If you had mostly c's*, you have a kinaesthetic learning style. You learn by touching and doing.
   - *If you picked two letters about the same number of times*, you depend on both of those learning styles.

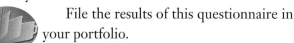 File the results of this questionnaire in your portfolio.

Activity 13

Working in Groups and Independently

Your teacher will time you for three minutes. During this time, create a list of musicians—solo artists or groups. Repeat the exercise, but this time do it with two or more of your classmates. Assign one of you to be the recorder. When you are finished, answer these questions on a sheet of paper:

1. Which activity did you prefer? Why?

2. In which situation were you most confident and comfortable?

3. In which situation were you most productive?

4. Think about other situations in which you have worked in a group and on your own. Apply questions 1 to 3 to these situations. You should be able to determine whether you prefer to work independently or in a group.

Write a summary about how you like to learn, and file it in your portfolio.

Your learning style is also influenced by whether you are **right-brained** or **left-brained**. Yes, you read that correctly. Studies have shown that each half of our brain serves a different function. The left half is logical, analytical, and used for language. The right half is used for creative thinking. This does not mean you use only half your brain, but most people have one side that is dominant.

Activity 14

Are You Right-Brained or Left-Brained?

Read each question. On a sheet of paper, write down the question number and an "a" or a "b" for the answer that you would most likely choose.

1. Which is more true of you?
   a. I am tense about getting things right
   b. I am relaxed and let things happen

2. Which do you enjoy more about music?
   a. the beat
   b. the melody

3. Which way of learning do you like best?
   a. books and lectures
   b. workshops and field trips

4. Which of these two subjects do you like more?
   a. math
   b. art

5. When you buy something, do you make sure you have received the correct change?
   a. yes, I count it
   b. no

6. How do you figure things out?
   a. a piece at a time, then put it all together
   b. the answer comes to me all at once, like a light going on

7. Which would you rather do?
   a. read
   b. watch TV

8. How are you at putting your feelings into words?
   a. very good
   b. it is hard for me

9. If you practise an instrument or a sport, how do you do it?
   a. the same time each day, for a certain amount of time
   b. when I feel like it and have the time

10. You are riding your bike to a friend's house. You have never been there before. Which method do you use to find your way?
    a. I ask for directions, then write down street names and landmarks
    b. I ask for directions, then look at a map

11. Which of these types of fabrics do you prefer?
    a. fabrics without much texture (cotton, denim)
    b. fabrics with lots of texture (corduroy, suede, velvet)

12. Are you good at remembering faces?
    a. no
    b. yes

13. Are you good at remembering names?
    a. yes
    b. no

14. How do you feel about psychic claims—that there is such a thing as ESP (extrasensory perception), for example?
    a. they are foolish and non-scientific
    b. science cannot explain everything; they are worth looking into

Total your a's and b's. Left-brained responses are a's; right-brained responses are b's.
- *Twelve or more a's or b's* means you strongly prefer that side of your brain.
- *Nine a's or b's* means you somewhat prefer that side of your brain.
- *Seven of each* means you use both sides of your brain equally.

Identify which side of your brain you use most.

 File the results of this questionnaire in your portfolio.

"Your Honor, he was driving his car using the left side of his brain, while his license indicated he was only to drive with the right side!"

If you are right-brained, does that mean you are never logical? If you are left-brained, does that mean you are never creative? Of course not. All it means is that you tend to favour one side over the other. It is just part of your personal style.

Activity 15

Which Side Is in Control?

Which side of your brain controls most of your activities? Find out with this simple exercise. Remember that the left side of your brain controls the right side of your body, and the right side of your brain controls the left side of your body. Write down your responses (R or L) on a separate sheet of paper numbered 1 to 5.

1. Clasp your hands together. Which thumb is on top?

2. Fold your arms. Which arm is on top?

3. Cross your legs. Which leg is on top?

4. Look through a paper tube. Which eye do you use?

5. Kick a ball. Which foot do you use?

   Which side of your brain is in control?

   There are many interesting approaches to figuring out who you are. By completing these activities you will become more self-knowledgeable, more self-confident, and more aware of your strengths and weaknesses.

PORTFOLIO

Creating a Personal Summary

Create a personal summary of each section of this chapter—your intelligences, true colour or personality type, whether you are left- or right-brained, a group or independent learner, and what your learning style is. Give an example that demonstrates each category.

JOURNAL

Expanding on Your Personal Profile

Reflect on how the information you have learned in this chapter has added to your picture of who you are. Has this information changed your outlook about people you know? If so, how? Write a few paragraphs describing your observations in your journal.

Looking Back

1. How will knowing the types of intelligence you have help you choose options at school and career possibilities for the future?

2. Why is your emotional quotient an important part of your personal make-up?

3. How will knowing your personality type help you select activities inside and outside school?

4. Will knowing what type of learner you are change the way you prepare for a test or a presentation? How?

5. How will being a group learner or an independent learner influence your choice of careers and specific jobs?

EXPLORATIONS

Reflections

Write a letter to a teacher from your past, outlining what you now know about your learning style.

Action!

Form groups and determine which types of intelligences are represented in it. Volunteers can assume different intelligences if all the intelligences are not represented in the group. Each student will role-play a cartoon-like superhero that exaggerates one aspect of that type of intelligence.

Featuring. . .

Advice Column: Give advice on how teens of different "true colours" can be friends.

Editorial: Write an editorial on the importance of self-knowledge.

Personal Story/Interview: Does your community give awards to people who are outstanding citizens? Does your school give awards for active involvement in your school, for achievement in academics, music, or athletics? Write the story of someone who has an exceptional talent. You might want to focus on what it is like to be that way and what were the first signs that he or she had this special quality.

Research: Look into other formal methods that can be used to assist a person in answering the question "Who am I?" such as handwriting analysis, numerology, horoscopes, or palm reading. Or investigate one of the following: what emotions are associated with certain colours, what certain colours symbolize (for example, purple is linked to royalty), what effects certain colours have on people.

Advertisement: Create an advertisement for one of the psychological inventories you have explored in this chapter, such as intelligence types, personality types, or learning styles.

Setting Personal Goals

· ·

What You Will Learn

- The reasons for setting goals.
- What goals are.
- How to set goals.
- How to evaluate your progress in achieving your goals.

Terms to Remember

goals	short-term goal
action plans	long-term goal
self-esteem	meaningful goals
reachable goals	creative visualization

Now that you have a clearer idea of who you are, it is important that you continue to grow, and develop your strengths and abilities. As well as asking yourself the question "Who am I?" ask yourself these questions: "Where am I now? Where am I going? How am I going to get there?" **Goals**, or where you want to get to, help you realize that there are things you can do yourself, and that you can make things happen. Translating dreams into specific goals, and goals into **action plans**, is essential for personal growth. Setting goals and striving to achieve them is taking action. Action raises your **self-esteem**, or your opinion of yourself. Set a goal and start doing everything you can to achieve it. Goals give order and direction to your energy.

DREAM

ACTION PLAN
• take drama classes
• job shadow at the local TV station
• figure out how to interview a TV personality
• study television shows—why I like/do not like them
• join a theatre group or school play

GOAL

What Is a Goal?

A goal is something you want to accomplish. For this reason, a goal should be **reachable** or doable. Do not set a goal that is close to impossible to achieve. There are both short-term and long-term goals. A **short-term goal** could be to take better care of your pet, starting today. A **long-term goal** could be to finish high school. Short-term goals, such as getting an A on your next test, often lead to long-term goals, such as graduating to the next grade. Be realistic about who you are and what your strengths and abilities are. A goal should also be **meaningful**. It should move you toward improving yourself. It should agree with your values. Goals are set to help you on your journey to success.

How to Set Short-Term Goals

1. Decide on your goals and list them. Set only three to six at a time so you can reach them. List only those goals you want, not those you think others expect of you. Make sure your goals are achievable and meaningful. Will they help you manage your life in a positive way?

2. Develop a workable action plan to achieve your goals. Create small, manageable steps that build toward reaching your goal.

3. Evaluate your progress—are you completing the action steps? Have you accomplished your goals? After analyzing how you are doing, you might need to revise your goals and action steps. Do not be afraid to make mistakes. Learning from mistakes can help you keep growing.

Setting Goals

4. Revise your goals and plans.

1. Decide on goals and list them.

3. Evaluate your achievement.

2. Develop an action plan to achieve goals.

Setting goals can be depicted by a circle, as shown at right.

Amin's Short-Term Goals

CATEGORIES	GOALS	ACTION STEPS
Friends	• improve friendship with two friends	• spend one night and one day a week with Nick and Leah • plan one activity every two weeks. Don't wait for them to call me
Family/Culture	• get along better with my family	• feed the dog every day • clean my room once a week • talk to my brother at least once a day
Health/Fitness	• improve my health • exercise more • become a better basketball player	• get more sleep • have junk food only once a week • bike to school • walk more • practise one night a week after school
Attitudes	• be more positive • use my time more productively	• stop myself when I am about to complain or make a face • remind myself what I do well when I start to criticize myself • keep trying. Don't get discouraged if something is hard at first • watch less TV • take swimming lessons
Helping Others	• do more with little kids	• ask to help with reading to the grade twos • help coach little league
School	• improve in science	• ask for help when I don't understand • do my homework every weeknight

Activity **1**

Creating Goal Categories

Study the short-term goals that Amin created. He selected the same categories that you worked with in Chapter 1 with the addition of "school." Working in groups of three, brainstorm other categories that could be added.

Activity **2**

Evaluating Amin's goals

A goal must be *reachable* and *meaningful*. Study the goals Amin has selected. For each goal, indicate whether it meets these two rules.

Developing an Action Plan

Sometimes goals might seem very general. They sound great, but can they be achieved? Developing a workable, manageable action plan is important to your success. Action plans must be very specific and detailed. Following many small steps is the easiest way to accomplish your goals.

Activity **3**

Analyzing Amin's Action Steps

Working with your group, examine the action steps that Amin created for each of his goals. Determine if some should be more detailed, and then record what the additional action steps should be. For example, Amin's goal to improve his health by getting more sleep might require that he add "go to bed at 9:30 p.m. instead of l0:30 p.m." to his action step.

Setting Your Short-Term Goals

To help you determine what you would like to accomplish, do some daydreaming. **Creative visualization** is a method of focussed daydreaming. It can help you with everything from your tennis game, to how well you relate to other people, to planning your future.

Activity 4

Take Time to Dream

1. Visualize what you think a perfect day would be. Start from when you wake up to when you go to bed. Include what you would like to do, not just what you do well. Let your mind create an image for each of the categories in Amin's goal organizer.

2. Next, outline in words or create a storyboard of what you think an ideal week would look like. It is easy to daydream and to make up a new life for yourself. To make it come true, you have to choose one small part of it and decide that is what you are going to try for first.

PORTFOLIO

Identifying a Goal

Write about something at which you would like to succeed. Why is it important? What happened when you tried before? What were the obstacles? What strengths do you need to succeed?

Activity 5

Testing Your Goal

In groups of three, one person states his or her goal. The second person assumes the role of the pessimist, or the negative person, and gives all the reasons the goal cannot be attained. The third person is the optimist, or the positive person, and encourages the goal-setter by offering solutions to problems created by the pessimist. Do this activity three times, each time changing the role you play.

Activity 6

Developing Your Personal Goal Organizer

1. Create a personal goal organizer similar to the one Amin designed. Are there categories from your brainstorming session in the first activity that you want to add to your organizer? Are there some categories Amin selected that you are not interested in?

2. In your organizer, record at least one short-term goal for each category.

3. Setting goals does not do much good if they are not put into action. Design an action plan with steps for each of your goals. Ask yourself "What do I need to do to get from here to there?" Make the steps as small and manageable as possible.

4. Keep your organizer in a place where you can see it several times a day; for example, on the mirror in your room, or in your binder. You might want to create a slogan, such as "Take Action!" or "One Step at a Time!" and put it on your locker door.

Evaluating Your Progress

Self-esteem comes when you know you have accomplished what you set out to do. If you do not meet your goals or follow your action plan for a day, a week, or even longer, do not give up. Pick up where you left off and try again. The following poem offers words of encouragement for when you are in a slump.

Never Give Up

My goals are set. My reach is far and strong

I aim for the highest star in my own sky.

Confidence is overflowing.

The key to success I hold tightly in my hand.

I start my journey.

But the star seems too high, the journey too tough.

Can I attain my dream?

My reach weakens but my arms are still outstretched.

I wipe my tears and flex my heart. I am stronger.

I won't give up.

Firmly in my grasp is the key—the key called perseverance.

—Erin Misener, Mount Albert, Ontario

If you are close to achieving your goal but cannot seem to reach it, you might need to figure out what else to try. Evaluate your action steps to determine if you are following them and decide if they are helping you to achieve your goal. One way to evaluate your progress is to maintain a Goals Journal.

J O U R N A L
Recording Your Goals

Create a journal with one page for each of your goals. Choose one or two goals to focus on. A sample journal page is pictured here, but you might wish to create your own style of journal. You could include mementos from your day with your journal entries, illustrate your day instead of writing about it, or use a cassette tape on which you could record your

My Goals Journal
Goal: Get along better with my family
Date: January 13
Action steps: I helped my younger brother by tying his skates for hockey.
How I feel: I was surprised by how we got along. We even joked a bit.

daily activities. Each night for the next week, record in your journal anything you did to help you accomplish your goals. Also record how you felt each day.

At the end of the first week, analyze how you are doing. Asking the opinion of others can help you to evaluate your progress. For example, Amin could ask his parents if they have noticed an improvement in his eating habits. Look at your goals. Is there someone—a family member, a friend, a teacher—who can give you feedback on how you are doing? Depending on the information you receive, you might want to make adjustments to your goals and your action steps. Or, you might find out that you have been successful!

For each goal, answer these questions:

1. Is there a goal for which you have no action steps?
2. Do you have a goal that has fewer entries than the others?
3. Are there some goals you have already achieved?
4. Are you taking the action steps you outlined but feel they are not helping you accomplish your goal?
5. Are there other resources you can use to help you analyze your action plan?
6. Is there more information you need about what you would like to do? Perhaps there is information in your school or public library, or you could search the Internet. With new information, you might have to adjust your action plan to make your goal achievable.

Evaluation might lead you to making some changes in your organizer. Depending on what your analysis of your Goals Journal tells you, you might have to add some action steps to achieve a goal, or you might have to revise a goal to make it reachable and meaningful. Do not get discouraged. Simply revise the plan to make it work for you!

Creating Action Deadlines

Have you ever postponed doing your homework until Sunday night even though you had all weekend to do it? Sometimes people approach their action plans the same way. One of Amin's action steps was to clean his room. His journal showed that he did not do this during the first week. Amin decided to add "every Thursday" to his action step. To avoid putting things off, put a specific time on your action steps. Do you need to add some deadlines to your action steps?

Continue with your Goals Journal for two more weeks. At the end of each week, analyze your situation and continue to make changes, if needed.

Because goal setting and action taking is critical to personal growth and self-esteem, continue setting new goals, developing action steps, and keeping a Goals Journal.

J O U R N A L

Reviewing Goals

What were the positive rewards you received from keeping your Goals Journal? What did you learn about yourself? What was the hardest action step to accomplish? What was the easiest goal to achieve? Will you continue to keep this journal? Why or why not?

Looking at Long-Term Goals

Achieving short-term goals builds confidence and self-esteem. Short-term goals can also serve as action steps to achieving long-term goals. It is not too early to start thinking about your long-term goals. Just going to school each day can be an action step toward a future goal. It might be an educational, career, personal, or social goal.

Activity 7

Creating Long-Term Goals

Choose one of Amin's short-term goals and turn it into an action step for a long-term goal or goals. Amin's short-term goal to improve his health could become an action step toward a long-term goal, such as becoming a nutritionist. Create long-term goals for Amin for each category.

Activity 8

Expressing a Long-Term Goal

Now it is your turn! Create a bumper sticker, a licence plate number, or a book title to express a long-term goal that you might have. Be creative! But remember, like short-term goals, long-term goals must be reachable and meaningful.

PROFILE

....

Kwantum Leap

Jenny Wai Ching Kwan is one of British Columbia's first Chinese-Canadian women elected to the B.C. Legislative Assembly. At 21, she had no idea what she wanted to do with her life. At 30, she is a successful politician. Kwan credits her success, in part, to a period of soul-searching that led her to discovering her purpose in life. After graduating from high school, she went on to study business administration at university, but found she really didn't have the interest. Still uncertain as to her direction, Kwan took a trip to Hong Kong and China "to find her roots." When she saw the overwhelming inequalities between the rich and the poor, it made Jenny realize what democracy means and how important it is. She also discovered a new-found pride in her ancestry.

Jenny returned to school, intending to become a lawyer. But a co-op placement in her last term introduced her to a variety of community groups. Realizing she could make changes outside the legal system, Jenny became a community advocate. "What became clear to me is that I wanted to ensure that the community had access . . . to the Charter of Rights and Freedoms." In 1993 Jenny was elected to City Council for Vancouver. In 1996 she ran and won in the provincial election.

In setting and achieving goals, Jenny advises that the basis must be passion and commitment. "You've got to be interested in what you're doing. If you don't know what it is you want to do, then take your time to search for that." In the process, advises Jenny, you must listen to your own instincts.

People tried to discourage her from making the trip to Hong Kong and China. "When you know what it is that you need to do, the amount of self-confidence and esteem you build into what you're doing is enormous. . . . The next step is to find out how to translate your ideas into action."

Jenny believes that "there's still a lot of change that I'd like to see. . . . Equality and justice are the essence of what I live for."

Reprinted with permission from *Career Paths* 1996, published by YES Canada–BC and funded by Human Resources Development Canada and the BC Ministry of Education, Skills, and Training.

1. How often did Jenny change her direction before finding her number-one goal?

2. What is Jenny's attitude toward making changes?

3. What personal characteristics does Jenny have that help her to achieve her goals?

JENNY KWAN'S SIX STEPS TO GOAL SETTING

✓ 1. LISTEN TO YOUR INSTINCTS.

✓ 2. TURN IDEAS INTO ACTION.

✓ 3. BUILD A SUPPORT NETWORK.

✓ 4. SET A TIME FRAME

✓ 5. BE FLEXIBLE.

✓ 6. TRY, TRY AGAIN.

PORTFOLIO

Representing Yourself in the Future

Find a video clip, a photograph in a magazine or newspaper, or create your own drawing that represents what you will be doing for a career and what you will be like as a person in the future. You determine when the future is. It could be one year or ten years from now. With the image, write a description of your career and personal goals and list the action steps that you will need to follow to achieve your long-term goal.

Before you begin, read the following excerpt for inspiration!

You're Allowed

• To believe there are no limits to your own potential.

• To expect great things for yourself.

• To think and feel that you have the power to go for your own dreams and goals.

• To discover the unlimited potential within you.

• To think and feel you have the power within to change your life circumstances if you are not satisfied.

• To enjoy life.

— Barry Davis

Looking Back

1. Why must goals be reachable and meaningful?

2. Give an example of a short-term goal and a long-term goal.

3. List three action steps you would take to achieve the short-term goal of taking better care of your things.

4. What is self-esteem? Give an example of something that gave you positive self-esteem.

EXPLORATIONS

Reflections

Write a poem or song, or draw a picture, using the theme "Pursuing Your Dreams."

Action!

Review your Goals Journal. Decide if there is an entry in your Goals Journal you would like to share with the group. Select a meaningful entry that you could act out. Feel free to add to it, if necessary!

Or

In pairs, present the following scenario. One of you plays the role of a student without goals. The other acts as a peer tutor who wants to help the student decide on a goal and an action plan for it. Select a goal from one of the categories in your Personal Goal Organizer.

Featuring . . .

Advice Column: Write advice to parents/guardians of students who are without goals.

Research Article: Conduct a survey of your classmates. Ask them if they would be willing to tell you their number-one goal. Report on the survey findings and any conclusions you have reached.

Advertisement: Create an advertisement on the importance of setting goals.

Editorial: Write about the importance of goal setting for teens.

Personal Story/Interview: Interview a teacher in your school. Ask what goals he or she has set and accomplished.

Discovering Pathways

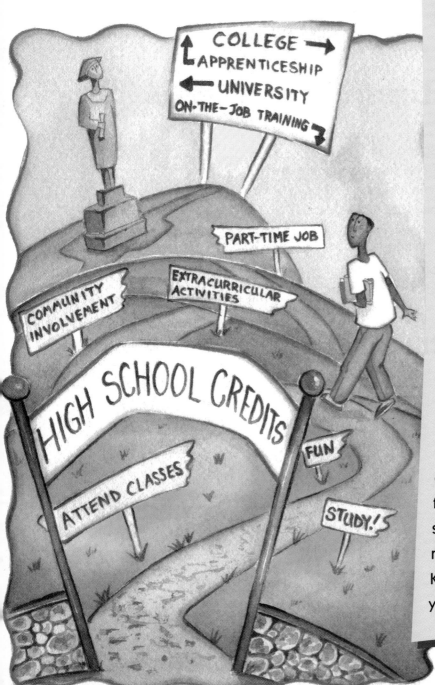

Making decisions about your future involves exploring different pathways. Now that you have a good understanding about yourself and know how to set goals, you can begin to determine where you are heading.

Some decisions will need to be made sooner than others. Choosing which high school courses to take is more important at the moment than making choices about education after graduation. Choosing volunteer activities or part-time work needs to be explored before making decisions about careers and full-time employment. Yet, what you do now affects decisions you will make later. For example, volunteering to assist in the primary grades could help you decide to work with children as a future career. If you work in a clothing store, you might decide that retail is not what you want to do in the future! Knowing all your options is essential as you start down the path to your future.

Education and the Job Market

What You Will Learn

- What to expect when in high school.
- Types of high school programs and subjects that are offered.
- What options you have if you cannot attend school full-time.
- About apprenticeships and youth apprenticeships.
- The differences among college, university, and other educational institutions.
- What post-secondary institutions are located in your local community, your province, and in other provinces.

Terms to Remember

alternative education programs
credits
mandatory
optional
semester
term
co-operative education
work experience
community service
youth apprenticeship

correspondence courses
independent learning courses
distance education
secondary
post secondary
apprentice
trade
diploma
degree

Education constantly increases in importance as the workplace continues to change. You need more education to give you more job choices and flexibility in the job market. There is a direct relationship between education and work in terms of job availability and job satisfaction. A lack of education limits a person's job choices and often leads to job dissatisfaction.

By the year 2000:

- The minimum requirement for 80 percent of jobs will be a high school diploma. This means that only 20 percent of jobs will be available for workers without a high school diploma.
- Without high school, you will be unemployed for 35 percent of your life. Entry into the better-paying jobs will continue to be severely limited for such workers.
- Of the 80 percent of jobs requiring a high school diploma, 50 percent will require five years of education beyond high school. This means 17 years of education, training, or on-the-job experience with training.
- In the growth areas, 90 percent of jobs will require college, university, or other educational training.

Education and the Job Market

High School

We know that high school is mandatory, or required, until you are 16. We also know that it is important for employment. But what do you currently know about high school? Where did you get your information—from a brother, a sister, or older friends? As you have learned, you are an individual, and the experiences of others will not be the same for you. Every person and every community is different. To discover what your high school education could be like, you need to ask a lot of questions and get solid answers from those who know.

What is the best advice a new high school student could receive?

- Use every opportunity to learn in the classroom and participate in extra-curricular activities.
- Ask questions and listen carefully to the answers.
- Look for a challenge and always try to do more than the minimum required.
- Take advantage of facilities such as the gymnasium and the resource centre or library.
- Make friends. High school friendships might last the rest of your life.

Before you begin high school or if you are unhappy with your high school, you need to gather a great deal of information. Consider the following topics.

Location: Do you have a choice of schools? Some communities are large and have several high schools that you could attend. You need to know what is available. For example, one school might specialize in the arts, while another might feature technology and science. Choosing a school because that is where your friends are going is very appealing, but you must look at your interests, skills, and abilities. Choose the school that has the best opportunities for you.

Alternative programs and schools: Are there **alternative education programs** available? Some communities offer schools that vary from the traditional structure. For example, an alternative school might be designed for independent learners who require a less formal structure. Also, traditional schools might offer alternative programs, such as enrichment programs for students who excel in science and technology.

Credits: A high school diploma requires a certain number of **credits** be earned. Some of these credits are **mandatory** (you must take them) and the rest are **optional** (you have a choice of which ones you want to take). Each credit can also be thought of as a subject or a class. For example, eight credits usually translates to eight different subject classes you take in school. The number of hours required for a credit varies from province to province. The number and type of credits required for graduation also varies from province to province. Find out your provincial requirements. How many of each subject are required? What are the mandatory credits? How many credits must you take in one school year? Are these credits available at more than one level of difficulty?

A credit can be earned at different levels of difficulty. Which level you choose depends on your education and career goals. You must know what the differences in the credits are, what the names of the levels are, and what your options are upon completion of the credits.

Program focus: You have already discovered your areas of strength and ability and might have an idea of the career area you would like to pursue. The optional subjects should be examined with this in mind to help you follow your career pathway. For example, if you are musically intelligent, what courses are available? What is the physical education program like if you are bodily intelligent? If you are language intelligent, how many language courses are available beyond what is required?

Career education: You have started on your career path. There is more to learn before you make some final decisions. What career preparation courses and career guidance counselling are available?

Extra-curricular activities: There are many activities that take place before and after school; for example, sports, music and drama productions, travel opportunities, clubs (language, chess, computers, photography), student council, athletic council, dances, concerts, school newspaper, and school yearbook. Which ones that interest you are available?

Schedule: There is a variety of schedules on which a school might choose to operate. A two-semestered system divides the year into two equal parts, or **semesters**. Your school might be on a four-**term** schedule. Another schedule is a full school-year. Which schedule does the school that you will be attending, or are attending, use? If you have a choice of schools you can attend, and they are each on a different schedule, what are the advantages or disadvantages of each one?

Transportation: How will you get to school? Will you walk? Are you eligible to take a school bus? When you are able to drive yourself, are there restrictions?

Fees: There are some costs involved in attending high school; for example, lockers, books, special equipment, student council fees, athletic fees, yearbook, and so on. Find out how much these items cost.

Community-based learning: Many high schools now have a broad connection with the community. Are there opportunities for you to gain credits for learning that occurs outside the classroom? Are there **co-operative education** or **work experience** opportunities? Is there mandatory **community service** as a requirement for graduation? Are **youth apprenticeship** programs offered?

Activity 1

Gathering Data

There are many sources for finding the information you need. With your teacher and classmates, decide which ones appeal to you.

- Every high school has a program/course description booklet. Ask the schools in your community to send copies to your class.
- Invite a student from a co-operative education or work experience program, and a student from a youth apprenticeship program, to speak about their experiences.
- Ask last year's graduates from high schools to participate in a panel discussion about their high school experiences.
- Attend information sessions offered by the high schools.

- Organize a parent/guardian information night at your school and ask representatives from the high school(s) to attend.
- Ask a guidance counsellor from a high school to speak to your class.
- Take a tour of a high school.
- Many boards of education have information on a web site on the Internet. Use the Internet and share your findings with the class.

Design a chart similar to the following. Add other categories that you want to know about. Take the questionnaire with you as you gather the information.

Preparing for High School

Name of School:			
Location:			
Alternative Programs:			
Credits Required - mandatory: - optional:			
Program Focus (optional subjects):			
Career Education:			
Extra-Curricular Activities:			
Schedule:			
Transportation:			
Fees:			
Community-Based Learning:			

Activity 2 ●●

Analyzing Data

1. If you have a choice of high schools to attend, list the advantages and disadvantages of each one. Which one will you choose and why?

2. You have gathered a lot of information about high school. List what appeals to you the most about your future school. List any concerns you have about it.

3. If you have a choice of subjects in your first year, list the ones you would like to take, or are taking. Why did you choose them?

JOURNAL

Visualizing High School

Visualize your high school years. What do you want to accomplish? What subjects would you still like to take? Will you participate in other extra-curricular activities? Will you develop new friendships? Describe your visualization in your journal in words, drawings, or on tape.

Alternative Ways to Complete Your Education

Not everyone can attend high school full-time due to a variety of reasons—the need to work, poor health, or family responsibilities. For others, the traditional route just might not appeal to them. There are numerous options available:

• Alternative education programs (described earlier) might enable you to attend school on a flexible time schedule.

• You can attend school by taking night school and summer school courses.

• In **correspondence courses** or **independent learning courses**, study materials are mailed to you to complete at home. You then return your work by mail to be marked. Once you have completed all the course requirements, you receive a diploma.

• **Distance education** involves using computer connections and telephone conference calls. You communicate with an instructor and classmates to complete course requirements. Some courses are also available over the radio.

• Youth apprenticeships combine in-school learning and on-the-job training. See the following section for more information.

Youth Apprenticeships

Would you like to be a plumber, a hairstylist, or a motorcycle mechanic? Many schools across Canada offer youth apprenticeship programs starting in Grade 11. You can train for a career while still in high school, with work-site learning and a paycheque from the employer. When you graduate, you continue working toward your goal.

Some of the more common careers available through youth apprenticeships are:

- glazier
- electrician
- tool and die maker
- small-engine mechanic
- auto body repairer
- automotive painter
- fuel and electrical systems mechanic
- heavy duty equipment mechanic
- plumber
- general machinist
- industrial woodworker
- pattern maker
- steam fitter
- painter and decorator
- mould maker
- cook
- automotive machinist
- farm equipment mechanic
- motor vehicle mechanic
- sheet metal worker
- general carpenter
- ironworker
- hairstylist
- fitter (structural steel/plate work)

IN THE NEWS

When Normal High School Is a Bad Fit

by Todd Mercer

Julie Lee became a self-described skipaholic when she was in Grade 10. Her A marks fell and she dropped out. "I took a year off, worked, got laid off. I didn't want to go back to school because my friends would be graduating and I'd still be in Grade 10." Instead, Lee enrolled in an alternative school. She admits to goofing off her first year, but "eventually you realize you're not getting any younger."

Like mainstream high schools, the alternative schools offer core subjects from Grade 10 through to graduation. However, they deliver these courses without formal classes or daily attendance requirements. This flexible scheduling particularly serves the needs of mature students who have other demands on their time, such as a job or children. Students must see each subject teacher at least ten hours during the course, usually in half-hour appointments once a week. The one-to-one tutorial meetings are key to learning. The learning is self-paced. Students can work intensely to complete a course over four or five months or, if their schedule demands it, over a longer period of time. Without the alternatives offered by such schools, many students claim they would simply drop out.

Reprinted by permission of Todd Mercer.

Students Gain a Better Understanding of the RCMP

In October 1995, G.P. Vanier Work Experience Co-ordinators Isabelle Pacholuk and Fiona Tayless and Constable Derek Kryzanowski of the Courtenay, B.C., Royal Canadian Mounted Police (RCMP) detachment launched the idea of a Mountie training camp (the first of its kind in Canada).

For six days 65 students lived in barracks and dressed in regulation RCMP uniforms, shirts pressed, shoes shined, and hats on. The day started at 5 a.m. and a few students managed to last until lights out at 11.

Based on the model of the Regina, Saskatchewan, RCMP training academy, drill, Cooper's Run, physical training, PARE testing, law classes, Deadly Decisions, traffic control, crisis intervention, firearms training, emergency response, underwater recovery, drug control, tracking with police dog, helicopter (rides for some!), and more drill (one student complained his brand new pair of shoes had no soles left after camp) were all part of the experience.

Twenty-five RCMP officers and 13 auxiliary members volunteered their time—240 volunteer hours. And what did they hope to get out of it? Constable Kryzanowski stated their objectives: give the students the opportunity to experience the training and working conditions of police officers, develop a better understanding and appreciation of the police, provide a

setting that enables officers and students to work together in a positive fashion, enhance students' self-esteem and leadership skills, and educate the public about positive youth/police contacts. Judging by the student evaluations, all of these goals and more were achieved. Their major complaint was that one week wasn't long enough!

On Sunday March 17th, 65 "green recruits" walked through the main gate, many of them looking like they doubted the wisdom of their choice. On Monday in parade square they looked like the misfits from *Hogan's Heroes*. However, on Graduation Day, Saturday March 24th, goose bumps ran down our arms, and tears of pride filled our eyes as our 65 young officers marched in unison and stood at attention before an emotional Constable Kryzanowski. This is what made one of the largest projects our work experience program ever tackled so worthwhile!

As we told our students on Graduation Day: "What you obtain by reaching your destination isn't nearly as important as what you become by reaching that destination!"

Due to the overwhelming success of this camp, both the RCMP and School District #51 ran a second training camp during spring break, March 1997.

Article written by Isabelle Pacholuk, Work Experience Co-ordinator at G.P. Vanier Secondary School in Courtenay, B.C.

Getting an Education Using the Internet

by Peter Giffen

When high school student Kerry Shipton discovered she could not take an English course last spring because of a timetable conflict, she decided to use the Internet. The 16-year-old phoned the government and arranged to do the course via e-mail.

"The whole thing was done over the computer," recalls her father, John Shipton, a French teacher. "She would receive an assignment one day, do it the next, and have it returned and marked on the following days. The whole process was fast and efficient. She polished off the course in ten weeks. She wouldn't even let me help her."

From "The Virtual Classroom" by Peter Giffen, Sympatico Netlife, Sept./Oct. '96

JOURNAL

Alternative Ways of Learning

Suppose that in the future you are unable to attend school full-time. In your journal, write what the advantages and disadvantages are of each of the alternative ways to get an education. Which type would best suit your learning style? Why?

After High School

High school is often called **secondary** education. *Post* means *after*. Therefore, **post secondary** means after high school. As you learned from the statistics at the beginning of this chapter, post-secondary education is very important for pursuing future career opportunities. Post-secondary education might seem like a long time away for you, but it is never too early to start thinking about the choices that are available. Post-secondary education can be achieved in a variety of ways—apprenticeships, on-the-job training, college, university, and private institutions.

To increase your options, you can gain more skills and further your education while working through apprenticeships and workplace training programs.

What Is an Apprenticeship?

If you do not enter a youth apprenticeship program while you are in high school, you can enter into an apprenticeship after graduation. While you are working, you are trained as an **apprentice**. This involves on-the-job training done by a qualified person, and it involves some time spent taking courses—usually at a college. The training is in a **trade** (a job or business involving manual or mechanical ability or buying and selling). This leads to jobs for men and women as skilled tradespersons. Apprenticeships are regulated by the government and, therefore, are well-recognized in industry.

Some of the advantages of becoming a skilled tradesperson are that, on average, wages for full-time positions are higher than in many other businesses or industries. There is a growing demand in Canada for tradespeople. Switching jobs when you are ready for a change is therefore easier. Depending on the career you choose, the hours you work, where you work, and the technology you use might vary a great deal. If you are looking for job flexibility, learning a trade might be one answer. The combination of learning in the classroom and hands-on learning in the workplace can be very appealing.

Colleges and Universities

The careers you are interested in might demand a college **diploma** or university **degree**. Colleges offer one-, two-, or three-year diploma courses. Universities offer three- or four-year degrees and offer post-graduate degrees called Masters and Doctorates.

Both university and college have registration costs of several thousand dollars. You might not have a college or university in your community. If this is the case, then the additional costs of either living away from home or driving a long distance add to the expense of post-secondary education. To help with these costs, student loans and bursaries, or grants, are available. Also, you might be able to win a scholarship.

One way to get information is to use the Internet and the World Wide Web. SchoolNet is a source of information about all colleges and universities in Canada. Also, every college and university offers information on all their courses, fees, admission requirements, and so on. Most post-secondary institutions hold special "open houses" and information nights.

Information is also available from bookstores, guidance offices, career centres, or university and college admissions offices. Former students have also written books giving their opinions about what is good and bad about their college or university. *Maclean's* magazine does a yearly analysis and rates the major universities.

Activity ③ •

Researching Colleges and Universities

Using a variety of sources of information, find:
• The location of the nearest college and university to you
• The names of colleges and universities in your province
     Choose one college or university, and gather as much information as you can about:
• Courses offered
• Tuition fees
• Admission requirements
• On-campus residences and housing

Other Educational Institutions

Post-secondary education is not limited to government-run colleges and universities. There is a vast number of privately run institutions that provide training for a variety of careers. These include computer training, business courses (accounting, word processing, desktop publishing, management), child care, health care (dental assisting, laboratory assisting), travel, dance, dramatic arts, hairdressing, cooking, languages, modelling, photography, theatre make-up, music, electronics, and even truck driving.

There is a fee to attend these schools. Course lengths vary from one month to several years. As with colleges and universities, you can apply for student loans and bursaries.

What Is Out There?
Here are some choices you have:
• Colleges of Applied Arts and Technology
• Private Vocational Schools
• Hospital-Based Programs (technicians, assistants)
• Universities
• Agricultural Colleges
• Colleges of Art and Design

PROFILES

Naimah Mohammed

Naimah Mohammed says she's excited about enrolling at junior high. Science fascinates the 14-year-old and she has narrowed her career choices down to pediatrician, pharmacist, or astronomer. "I like finding out about new things, especially about [outer] space," she said.

Naimah wants to be like her three older sisters. "They're really smart," she said, explaining that they graduated from university with science degrees. "They got married and had children, too," she added.

Visiting relatives in Trinidad on her own was the best part of her final year at public school. Naimah said it made her feel "more independent."

Margot Townson

Margot Townson thinks the class of 2000 "has to set goals." So the 14-year-old Grade 9 student is trying her best. She ranked in the top ten of her Grade 8 class, played trumpet in the school band, and sang alto in the choir. She has also won awards for soccer, cross-country running, and track and field. During the summer, she earned her Red Cross bronze medallion in swimming and volunteered as a leader-in-training at a children's camp.

She's thinking about being a dentist. "It seems complicated, challenging, and I like a challenge."

Sometimes she stays awake in bed "thinking about what's going on in the world."

Philip Edamura

Philip Edamura had an active summer after Grade 8. Several times a week during the summer he went mountain biking with buddies. He also ran 9 to 12 km with a group of boys and girls. "It's really challenging. There's a lot of technique involved," he said of the sport he took up two years ago. When he went to a hockey summer camp, Philip learned to water-ski. "That was the best," he said enthusiastically. "It was new to me . . . travelling at that speed, adding things like jumping." Philip joined the cross-country running team at his high school and hopes to run about 10 km, six days a week.

So far, his favourite subjects are English and art. "Art, I've always liked it. We're working on sketches with pencil, shapes, and shading." As for a future profession: "Architecture might be an interesting one," he said. "I think it will be harder than when my parents got jobs. It takes better grades to get into university."

James McCrodan

James McCrodan is trying out for the high school rugger team this fall. "I'm going to put myself forward and strive," he said. Gym and math tied as his favourite subjects and music hit a low note last year. The 14-year-old says he has "no clue" about a career yet, but is thinking of being a car salesperson. "It would be fun," said James, whose dad owns car dealerships. "I've always wanted to go up to somebody and sell them a car."

1. Write a profile similar to these ones about yourself.

Researching Educational Requirements for Your Career

Choose a career that interests you. What education will you need for that career? What high school courses prepare you for post-secondary education for that career? What courses must you take in college or university? Which college or university in your province offers these courses?

Use the information sources discussed in this chapter to answer these questions. File your findings in your portfolio.

Activity 4

Listing Other Educational Institutions

Look in the Yellow Pages of your telephone book under the heading Schools. Make a list of other educational institutions in your community. Select two or three that relate to a career or careers that interest you and contact these places for information. Find out the length of the courses, the fees involved, and whether you need particular high school credits to enroll.

Reviewing Your Research

Review the research you have completed on the post-secondary opportunities that are available in your community. Select three you researched that appeal to you the most. On a sheet of paper, list the reasons why you selected them.

Looking Back

1. Why is choosing the right high school so important?

2. Identify a career that interests you. List the extra-curricular activities you could join that relate to that career. Describe what skills you might gain from them.

3. What are the differences among college, university, and other educational institutions?

4. Would you continue your education if you could not attend a secondary school full-time? Why or why not?

5. List the advantages of an apprenticeship.

EXPLORATIONS

Reflections

Create a cartoon for the caption "Don't Drop Out."

Goals

What do you think your post-secondary education will be? Give reasons for your answer.

Action!

In pairs, act out one of the following situations:
- Education is important.
- Choosing a non-traditional school or program is a challenge.
- I got ahead and I did not have any education!
- Marks are not everything!

Portray different viewpoints, such as those of a parent, a teenager, or an employer.

Featuring. . .

Advice Column: Write letters of advice from the perspective of three people who graduated from your school ten years ago. These three people are writing to your magazine to give advice to students who are currently in school.

Research: Complete a cost comparison among a college, a university, and a private institution (admission fees, books, other fees).

Advertisement: Create an ad for an alternative school.

Editorial: Write about future trends in education.

Personal Story/Interview: Interview an adult about his or her opinion of education today. Then write an article that summarizes the interview.

Earning and Managing Money

What You Will Learn

- Various ways to earn money.
- How to be an entrepreneur.
- How to develop a business plan.
- How to set up a personal budget.
- How to set financial goals.
- About banking services.
- How to apply for a Social Insurance Number (SIN).

Terms to Remember

entrepreneur
networking
marketing
marketing strategies
start-up money
seed money
business plan
expenses
break even

profit
hourly wage
budgeting
income
compound interest
invest
interest rate
Social Insurance Number

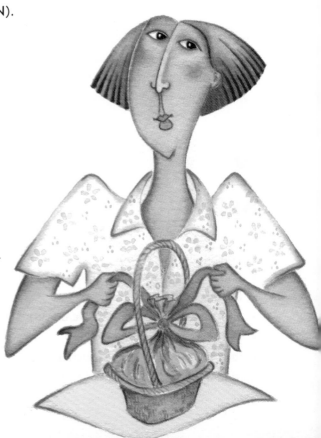

You have gone through many stages as you have grown from childhood to young adulthood, accomplishing major steps such as walking, talking, learning to ride a bike, and starting school. Each stage involves more and more responsibility. The first time you did a major project on your own, you probably felt pretty good about yourself. If you got paid for it, you probably felt even better!

As you grow from teenager to adult, your involvement in the work force will be ever increasing. You might begin by helping out and receiving a small reward for your time. Then, perhaps, you can build up a little business. Finally, as a teenager, you can seek part-time employment.

Many people love to work. They have found something they love to do and find personally rewarding. Working hard and doing a good job contributes to your self-esteem. You are kept busy and you feel needed and valued. As a young person, receiving payment helps you to become independent and enables you to purchase items and participate in activities that cost money.

Your First Job

Your first entry into the job market has, most likely, already happened. Have you done a small job for someone or made something for someone? Have you run an errand, or looked after younger brothers and sisters? After completing these jobs, you might have received some kind of payment in return. It might have been money or something you wanted.

In some situations, you might have done these tasks as part of your responsibility to your family. This is all part of growing up. Think of something you did for someone who is not in your family. As soon as you provide a service or product for someone and receive payment in return, you have become a member of the work force!

Activity 1

Identifying Your First Job

1. Think of your first job. Then, as a class, create a list of all the "first jobs" your class has had. Make a second list of the various payments that were received.

2. Ask several adults or older teenagers how they first entered the job market, and how they were paid. Are there any jobs that can be added to your class list? Were there some new forms of payment?

Working from time to time, or periodically, is thought of as doing "odd jobs." Once you do the jobs on a regular basis and they turn into a regular source of income, you are in business for yourself. For example, if you are a sitter on a regular basis, you can consider yourself to be in business for yourself. An **entrepreneur** recognizes an opportunity and assumes the risk to make it into a business. For example, if the occasional lawn-mowing job for your family has turned into mowing lawns for many of your neighbours, consider yourself an entrepreneur!

JOURNAL

Describing Your Favourite Odd Job

Describe your favourite odd job. Include details such as what you liked most about it, what you liked least, and how you were rewarded for your work. Draw a picture of the job or include a memento of it if you have one. Would you have enjoyed the job as much if you received only praise and thanks for a job well done?

Activity ②

Turning Odd Jobs into Self-Employment

Review the class list of first jobs. Write down the ones that could become a business, or be done on a regular basis, and would provide a regular source of income for young people.

You might wish to file the list in your portfolio.

PROFILE

An Eye Like a Spy

by Katherine Dodds

Bronwen Hughes

Bronwen Hughes doesn't fit the profile of a typical Hollywood director. Young, female, and Canadian, she's constantly searching for stories with strong women's roles. This 31-year-old director recently finished her first major motion picture, *Harriet the Spy*. Based on the 1964 children's novel by Louise Fitzhugh, the film chronicles the adventures of an eccentric 11-year-old who Hughes describes as someone who has her own way of doing things. So does Hughes, who has made her own path toward filmmaking. A competitive gymnast, then a teenage dancer, Hughes meant to become a photojournalist but somehow ended up a filmmaker. After years of directing commercials, documentaries, and music videos, she landed a gig with the Emmy-nominated Canadian comedy series *Kids in the Hall*, which proved to be her ticket to the big time—and the *Harriet* film. Hollywood now comes calling. Hughes describes her journey into directing and how she resembles Harriet.

"As a kid, I was such a *National Geographic* fan, I always thought of doing journalism or photojournalism. When it came time to visit Carleton University in Ottawa—the place for journalists—it was minus 40 degrees. I thought, 'I could never live here.' So I visited York University in Toronto. I had never been a film buff but had always taken photographs. It was almost like a calling. I just sort of swayed into film and got stuck.

"It's a dream come true to be directing a feature at all. But making a film is a very, very tough process. The director has to be ahead of everybody. There is so much demanded of a director, from the technical to the creative to the budgetary aspects. The stress is relentless. You have to be sure what you want because there is no time to change your mind.

"Some people will direct a feature of anything. But with every project you take, you define yourself as a director. The director *is* the film. First of all, you have to give a year of your life. Then, you wear it for the rest of your life. So doing something like *Harriet* as a first feature, I feel incredibly lucky. I find myself only interested in films with strong female leads, mostly adult versions of what Harriet is—people who go for what they want and overcome obstacles.

"When I started reading the script for *Harriet the Spy*, I thought, 'Here we go, another first-crush movie. . . .' But soon after that I realized Harriet wasn't doing any of the clichéd girl-movie, girl-story things. She didn't give one whit what the other people in the class thought about her. She wanted to be a writer and she did. That impressed me.

"I always took photographs—slice-of-life pictures. It was almost spy-like to get close to people and capture them when they least expected it. I started taking photographs in school art classes and mass-media assignments. In Grade 7, I started developing my own photographs. One of our assignments was to photograph our surroundings. A lot of kids took pictures of their family or their dog. But I crawled under the fence at the railway yard and took pictures of architecture and steam coming off the highrises. Those are the kind of details I would notice walking around or looking out the window of the family car. My parents might say, 'Ooh, that dirty yard,' but I saw a wealth of images or textures.

"I feel so good about having worked on *Harriet*, I'd love to find an adult version of the character. We have to come up with female role models that prove it's not just possible but necessary to express your feelings."

Originally printed in *Chatelaine*, March 1997. Reprinted, in an edited form, by permission of Katherine Dodds.

1. What skills did Bronwen acquire as a child that enabled her to change from being a *National Geographic* fan to studying film at York University?

2. What are the personal characteristics of Harriet? How does Harriet compare to Bronwen?

3. Create a teenage version of the character Harriet. For example, what would her personality be like and what activities would she be involved in? Incorporate the characteristics Bronwen admires.

Creating Your Business

You might have a great idea for a business, but without customers you will not succeed. A way to find customers is through **networking**. Make personal contacts with people you think will need what you have to offer. Then talk to everyone you know about your business and ask them to tell others. You might be surprised by the number of people who want your product or service!

Activity  3

Finding Customers

In groups of three or four, brainstorm who the customers would be for each of the businesses on the class list you developed earlier. Do the same for any activities on the following list that do not appear on your class list.

- Baby-sitting or setting up a baby-sitting agency
- Organizing a street sale in your neighbourhood
- Gift wrapping
- Planning birthday parties, or working as a clown at parties
- Jewellery making
- Computer-based work, such as creating flyers for garage sales

- Dog walking/bathing
- Collecting, fixing up, and reselling used items
- Snow removal service
- Gardening and/or lawn cutting
- Fence painting
- Window cleaning
- Growing your own seedlings and selling plants
- Grocery shopping
- Library book/video rental return service
- Gift-basket making

 You might wish to file a copy of this list in your portfolio.

How to Attract Customers

Attracting customers is called **marketing** your business. Marketing is the process of planning and implementing a strategy for the promotion, sale, and distribution of goods or services. Marketing involves a plan of activities for this purpose called **marketing strategies**. Making personal contacts with people you think will need what you have to offer, "word of mouth" advertising, and networking are four excellent ways of attracting customers, but there are others. For example, you might need to display or give away some free samples of your products so they can be seen by a lot of people. You could have product parties, inviting neighbours and friends to come and see (and buy) your goods. If you provide a service, you might get new customers by having a special "introductory" price for first-time users. The possibilities are endless!

Activity 4

Creating Marketing Strategies

With your group, brainstorm some marketing strategies for three of the business ideas from your class list or from the list in Activity 3.

You might wish to file a copy of these strategies in your portfolio.

What Will It Cost?

Some of the businesses will need equipment and supplies before they can get started. For example, if you are planning to sell baking, you will need to purchase the ingredients and have the utensils. A lawn-care business requires rakes, shovels, a lawn edger, and a lawn mower. There might be some things you can use from home. You might need to purchase other items. Other businesses might require only time and ability. Remember that you might also need money for your marketing strategies. Entrepreneurship programs for young people often provide **start-up money** or **seed money** to fund a project at the beginning.

Activity 5

Listing Personal Rewards

As a class, make a list of the positive aspects of working that do not include money.

IN THE NEWS

Tad's Tranquility Tapes

Tad Regehr, 12, liked the sounds of crickets, frogs, and birds on his family's farm in Alberta so much that he taped them. He then taped a thunderstorm and the patter of rain. "I used the tapes to go to sleep," he says. "I thought other people might like to do that, too." Then he got the idea of mixing all the sounds together. Using a start-up grant of $100 from an entrepreneurship program for young people, he sat in his living room surrounded by stereo systems, each playing a different tape. Using a microphone, he put all the sounds together on a master tape.

After creating his own packaging, Tad took his tapes to arts-and-crafts stores and convinced owners to stock them. In one year, he'd sold $300 worth of tapes at $10 each. His advice to other young entrepreneurs? "It was a good hands-on experience and I learned to be businesslike. The thing is to try and keep at it."

Canada Career Information Partnership, *Canada Prospects* and *Ontario Prospects* 1996–97.

Erin and Janalee—Hammock-Makers

Prince Edward Island students Erin Mulligan and Janalee Cameron, 13, became entrepreneurs when they were 11 years old. "We wanted to do something in the summer," says Erin, "and with the help of my dad came up with the idea of making hammocks." With $180 seed money from an entrepreneurship program for young people, they purchased fishing net, string, rings, and glue, and had special oak sticks made, with holes for threading.

Each hammock takes about a day to make. "If you make a mistake," Erin says, "you have to start again. That's frustrating." But their efforts paid off. Erin-Lee Creations has sold 14 hammocks for $70 each. "It's nice having your own money," Erin adds, "and when you show you can take responsibility, people trust you more."

Canada Career Information Partnership, *Canada Prospects* and *Ontario Prospects* 1996–97.

1. How did Tad and Erin and Janalee get their start-up money?

2. Why did they need the money?

3. Tad began his business with $100. Erin and Janalee received money from a special fund for young entrepreneurs. What can you do to get some start-up funds, sometimes called seed money? Is there funding available for young entrepreneurs in your community?

Creating a Business Plan

Keeping track of the costs of starting up and running a business is done by creating a **business plan**. It is a way of knowing how much money you spent, how much you took in from your customers, and how much is left over.

Consider the following business: For Molly McGoo's Exceptionally Great Cookies, the cost of each cookie was 65 cents. Molly arrived at this figure by adding up her **expenses**, or the cost of making the product. She then divided that number by the number of cookies she would be selling. This gave her the price she would need to **break even**, or cover her expenses. The final price of the cookie had to allow her net income to include a **profit**, which is the monetary difference between her expenses and the money from her sales. The price of the cookies had to be reasonable, so that people would buy them. At the same time, it had to be high enough to make it worth the time it takes to make them. The following is Molly McGoo's business plan.

Business Plan
Molly McGoo's Exceptionally Great Cookies

Product: Cookies

Competitive Difference: These cookies will be made with natural fruit sugars and calorie-reduced sweeteners, perfect for those who want a calorie-wise treat.

Market/Income Projection	
# of customers to start:	12
# of cookies each customer will buy:	24
How often each will buy:	
Aunt Sally	weekly
Mrs. Brown	weekly
Mom	weekly
Mrs. Indiligo	weekly
Grandma	twice a month
Aunt Denise	once a month
Mrs. Kavo-Langley	once a month
Total number of cookies each month:	600
Price of each cookie:	$ 0.65
Monthly projected income:	$390.00

Projected Expenses	
Cost of ingredients	$225.00
Electricity	none
Equipment Rental	none
Wages	none
Advertising	$ 10.00
Bags for the cookies (20 bags @ 10¢ ea.)	$ 2.00
Retail location	none

Net Income (projected income minus projected expenses) **$163.00**

If your business is providing a service that does not involve supplies or equipment, you have to determine a reasonable cost for your service—a price that will allow you to make money, but at a price your customers can afford. Start with what you think is a reasonable amount of money to earn in an hour, or your **hourly wage**. Then calculate how long it will take you to do the job. Multiply the two and you will have a good idea of what you will earn from most of the jobs. Or, you could tell your customers how much you will charge by the hour. When you first start, you might find that you have to adjust your rates. If you are charging too much, you will not have many customers!

Activity 6

Becoming an Entrepreneur

On your own or with a partner:

1. Decide on a business.

2. Create a business name.

3. Determine who your customers might be (young parents, senior citizens, neighbours, and so on).

4. Create marketing strategies.

5. Create a business plan.

6. Put your plan into operation.

What to Do with the Money

Imagine that your business is successful and you now have more money than you ever had before. You have many choices when deciding what to do with your money. You might want to save it, or spend it as soon as you get it. You might want to save for a while and then buy a special item. Your money might be needed to help out your family in purchasing essential items.

Planning what to do with your money is called **budgeting**. You need to determine your **income**, or the amount of money you earn, the amount you spend, the amount you save, and the amount you have left over. You could set a budget for varying lengths of time—one week, one month, one year. To prepare a budget, you predict what your expenses and income will be. Then you keep track of what actually happens with your money. At the end of the budget period, you compare the actual amount to the predicted amount.

My Personal Budget by Jake

INCOME	AMOUNT PER WEEK	TOTAL FOR ONE MONTH
Allowance	$ 10.00	$ 40.00
Odd Jobs	$ 5.00	$ 20.00
Self-Employment	$ 20.00	$ 80.00
Total	**$35.00**	**$140.00**

EXPENSES	AMOUNT PER WEEK	TOTAL FOR ONE MONTH
Entertainment	$ 5.00	$ 20.00
Video Rentals	$ 4.00	$ 16.00
Lunches	$ 20.00	$ 80.00
Magazines	$ 3.95	$ 15.80
Total	**$32.95**	**$131.80**
Income – Expenses = Spending Money	$ 2.05	$ 8.20

Activity ⑦

Setting a Budget

Create a budget for yourself, based on the preceding one. Use the same three-column structure and the headings, and then fill in your own sources of income and types of expenses.

Setting Financial Goals

Many people find it very tempting to spend all their money. They might save it for a while to buy a high-cost item, but then it is gone. Money experts recommend that people should save 10 percent of the money they earn. The money formula would be this:

Income – Expenses – Savings = Spending Money

Imagine that Jake's savings are $1 a month. His spending money would now be $7.20.

Jake decides he wants to purchase a CD player for $100. How long will it take Jake to save the money? (Hint: Divide the amount Jake has to spend each week minus his $1 savings into $100. The answer will be the number of weeks Jake will need to save $100.)

To see what can happen if you keep your savings in a bank or trust company, study the following chart.

Monthly Contribution

Invested for 5 years	$ 25	$ 50	$ 100
At 4% Interest*	$1663	$3326	$ 6652
At 8% Interest*	$1849	$3698	$ 7397
Invested for 10 years	$ 25	$ 50	$ 100
At 4% Interest*	$3694	$7387	$14 774
At 8% Interest*	$4604	$9208	$18 417

* Invested at the start of each month; interest is compounded monthly.

If you save $25 a month for 5 years, you could save $1663 because you would earn **compound interest** on your money. Interest is a percentage of money the bank pays you for letting them use or **invest** your money while it is in the bank. Without interest, you would save $1500. The higher the **interest rate** (the percentage per year of the amount borrowed), the more money you will make.

Banks and trust companies have many services for young people. There are a variety of accounts into which you can put your money. You can obtain bank-machine access. When you are older, you might be able to get a student loan from your bank to help you attend a post-secondary institution.

Activity 8

Researching Banking Services

1. As a class, list the different types of banks in your community. Form groups, and have a volunteer from each group contact each bank. Explain the information you need and set up an appointment with a representative. While you are there, gather as much information and as many printed materials as possible.

2. Many Canadian banks have information on the Internet about what they offer their customers, including young people. Search the Internet and collect as much student banking information as you can find.

3. As a class, have each group present the information it obtained. Compare what is available from each bank by creating a master list on bristol board.

banking at a glance

daily interest account

student budgeting software

student loan

Activity 9

Setting Goals

Decide on something you want or need. In your notebook, copy the following questions and answer them yourself.
• What do I want?
• How am I going to get it?
• Who or what can help me?
• What is going to get in my way and how will I deal with it?
• What do I have to give up?
• When can I work towards my goal?
   Are some changes needed in your budget? How long will it take before you can buy what you want?

Your First Part-Time Job

As you grow older, you might find that your small-business activities and odd-job way of earning money are not enough. Or, you might want to try something new. You decide it is time to work for someone else on a regular basis, after school, on weekends, or during the summer. One important fact is that you must be 14!

You can get ready for part-time employment by applying for a **Social Insurance Number (SIN)**. This is a nine-digit number used by the federal government to identify people. It is issued on a wallet-size plastic card. Everyone in Canada must have an SIN to be employed. The SIN is not needed to apply for a job. But, once you have a job, you must apply for your number within three days. Get one now and be prepared. Follow these easy steps:

1. Pick up an application form from the Canada Employment Centre nearest you. If you are not sure where it is, look it up under Federal Government in your telephone book.

2. Take one of the following documents with you:
   - Canadian provincial birth certificate
   - Certificate of birth and baptism (only for persons born and baptized in Newfoundland and Quebec)
   - For Registered Indian: If you wish to have your status in Canada recorded as "Registered Indian," you must provide your Certificate of Indian Status.
   - Canadian Immigration Record and visa or Record of Landing
   - Immigration form entitled Visitor Record or Employment Authorization or Student Authorization
   - Refugee Status Claim

3. Complete the application form and hand it in at your nearest Employment Centre.

4. In three to six weeks, you will receive your SIN and card.

JOURNAL

Describing What You Learned

Imagine that it is five years from now and you are looking back on your first experiences in the work force. What are your best memories of the experiences?

PORTFOLIO

Summarizing Your Work Experience

Write a summary of the various odd jobs you have done of which you felt particularly proud. If you are an entrepreneur, describe your business and your business plan. Include samples of the marketing strategies you used and, if possible, samples of your work, or pictures of it.

Looking Back

1. Give three reasons why people work.

2. What is the difference between doing odd jobs and being an entrepreneur?

3. List three marketing strategies.

4. What is a business plan?

5. Why should you save money?

6. List the rights and responsibilities of both employers and young workers.

EXPLORATIONS

Reflections

What is the value of work? Does it change as you grow older?

Goals

How can you increase your income? Determine the goals and action steps required to accomplish this. For example, in Activity 6 you "created" a business. Can you make it a reality or is there something else you would like to do? For example, you might want to increase the number of customers you currently have. How will you do this? Make a plan.

Action!

In your group, act out different scenes involving dealing with customers. You might want to demonstrate how to sell a product or service, how to handle an unhappy customer, or how to deal with a customer who will not pay.

Featuring. . .

Advice Column: Write columns that advise young people on how to earn money, set up a budget, and save money.

Advertisement: Create ads for some of your classmates' businesses.

Research: Research the spending and saving habits of teenagers in Canada. You might wish to contact the Canadian Bankers' Association or the CBC television program *Streetcents* web site.

Editorial: Write an editorial on "Young People Are Industrious!"

Personal Story/Interview: Write a feature about a young person in your community who is an entrepreneur.

Career Choices and Changes

What You Will Learn

- The four career clusters.
- The characteristics of each cluster and how to match the best one to you.
- How education affects career choice.
- Where to find information on careers.
- A job that interests you in your community.
- Future career trends.
- New ways of working.
- The impact of technology on the workplace.
- Jobs that are growing or declining.

Terms to Remember

futurist	job
demographer	cluster
career	trends

There will be many exciting opportunities for you when you are ready to enter the work force. The challenge is to keep up with the many changes that are occurring at an ever-increasing rate. Changes are occurring for several reasons:

- Computers and other technologies. Current jobs are replaced with new ones. Robotics and the Internet are two examples of how the way in which work is done is constantly changing. Business is no longer limited to one's own country; the world is available to all.
- Data, knowledge, and information are the new products of the workplace.
- The changing needs of people. The aging population of Canada affects what people buy, do, and use.

Some people wish there were a crystal ball that could tell exactly what the future will hold. In its place, however, there are ways that predictions are made about the future. For example, **futurists** specialize in watching what is currently happening, observing what changes are starting to occur, and predicting what will happen in the future. **Demographers** study the population of a country and determine what the future needs and actions of the population will be. It is important to study the predictions of futurists and demographers. You need to direct your talents, abilities, and energies down the right path.

In this chapter, you will study career clusters and some of the occupations that are available in each cluster. Future trends in careers and ways of working will also be examined.

You might know exactly what you want to be, or maybe you cannot decide. Either way, you have to find a good match between yourself and the constantly changing world of work. In this chapter, you will begin the process of career planning.

Career Clusters

All **careers** in our society can be categorized under four main headings. The **jobs** in each group, or **cluster**, require the same interests and abilities. The four clusters are:

- Communication and the Arts
- Engineering, Industrial, and Scientific Technology
- Health, Human, and Public Services
- Business and Marketing

You have learned a great deal about your abilities, personality, skills, intelligences, and goals. As you consider future career possibilities, you need to think about those that fit well with all your characteristics. Now you can start to focus on careers that will best suit you.

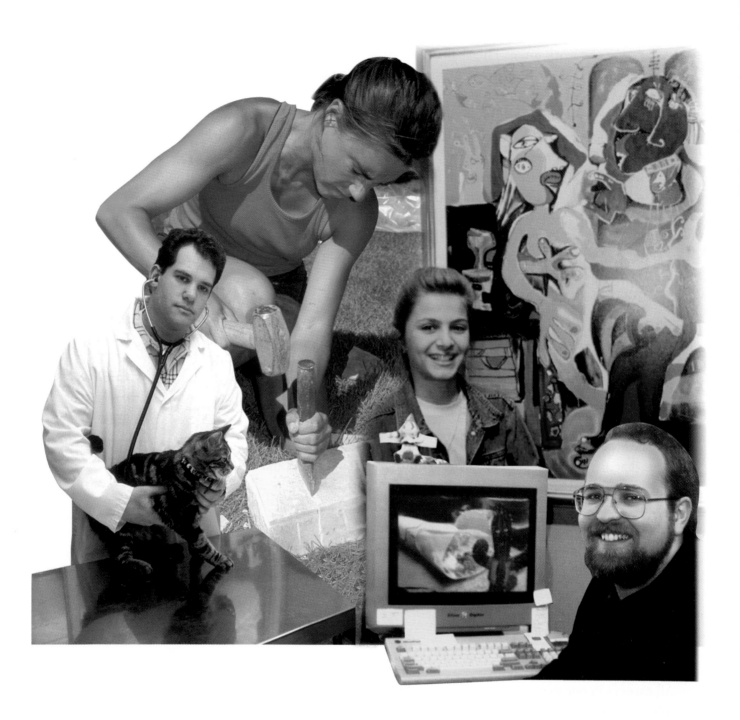

Activity ①

Describing Unfamiliar Jobs

The following Career Clusters chart lists the types of jobs that can be found in each cluster. For each career cluster, read the jobs that are listed. Write down any jobs that you have never heard of or that are unfamiliar to you. As a class, help one another describe these unfamiliar jobs. Make a list on the board and then, together, describe the jobs.

Career Clusters

COMMUNICATION AND THE ARTS	ENGINEERING, INDUSTRIAL, AND SCIENTIFIC TECHNOLOGY	HEALTH, HUMAN, AND PUBLIC SERVICES	BUSINESS AND MARKETING
• musician • artist • actor • dancer • choreographer • interior designer • fashion designer • costume designer • set designer • writer • publisher • multimedia expert • reporter • curator • photographer • make-up artist • editor • producer • director • agent • TV and radio announcer	• environmental planner • surveyor • software engineer • computer programmer • plumber • contractor • builder • miner • logger • landscape architect • aerospace engineer • inspector • machinist • mechanic • auto body technician • mason • electrician • electrical engineer • diagnostic technician • researcher • robotics expert	• home health-care worker • physician • educator • religious leader • child-care provider • psychologist • dentist • dental assistant • police officer • speech therapist • nurse • dietitian • veterinarian • emergency medical technician • physical therapist • biomedical technician • caterer • restaurant worker • cosmetologist • hotel manager	• purchasing agent • travel agent • store owner • advertiser • sales associate • market researcher • office manager • loan officer • stockbroker • accountant • economist • personnel manager • systems analyst • meeting planner • buyer • image consultant • comptroller

Activity ②

Listing "Smarts" and Career Clusters

1. With a partner, list the types of smarts that would be needed for success in each of the career clusters listed in the chart. (See pages 15-20 to review the types of smarts.) For example, jobs in Communication and the Arts would require word and picture smarts. What other smarts would be useful for this category? Add them to your list.

2. Which career cluster includes the greatest number of smarts that you possess?

3. Are there other similarities within each cluster, such as working for others or for yourself or working in large institutions or outside? List any similarities you find.

In addition to being categorized in career clusters, jobs can be classified under three main types. There are jobs that involve: working with people, working with information, and working with things. Each career cluster contains all three of these classifications.

Activity 3

Playing the Job Trek Game

On a sheet of paper, write down the number of each statement that describes you well. When you have finished, match up the numbers you picked with the number groups following the statements.

1. I would rather make something than read a book.

2. I enjoy problem-solving games and working at puzzles.

3. I like helping people when they need it.

4. I enjoy learning about new topics by reading about them.

5. I like working with my hands.

6. I like being the leader in a group of people.

7. I prefer to know all the facts before I tackle a problem.

8. I like to take care of other people.

9. I enjoy designing, inventing, and creating things.

10. I enjoy expressing myself through art, music, and writing.

11. I would like a job that lets me deal with people all day.

12. I like working with materials and equipment.

13. I enjoy learning new facts and ideas.

14. I find that co-operating with others comes naturally to me.

15. I like finding out how things work by taking them apart.

16. I would choose working with machines rather than working with people.

17. I can usually persuade people to do things my way.

18. I enjoy building and repairing things.

19. I enjoy the research part of my projects.

20. I like interacting with people.

21. I enjoy thinking up different ideas and ways to do things.

22. I like hearing other people's opinions.

23. I enjoy learning how to use different tools.

24. I find it easy to follow written instructions.

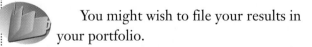 You might wish to file your results in your portfolio.

1, 5, 9, 12, 15, 16, 18, 23

Things are your thing.
You enjoy:
• Using tools and machines.
• Making objects with your hands.
• Maintaining or fixing equipment.
• Finding out how things work.

Jobs related to things are found in:
• Engineering
• Product manufacturing
• Construction
• Repair and servicing
• Transportation
• Trades and technology

3, 6, 8, 11, 14, 17, 20, 22

People are your pastime.
You enjoy:
• Caring for or helping others.
• Persuading people or negotiating.
• Working as part of a team.
• Leading or supervising others.

Jobs related to people are found in:
• Health care
• Education and training
• Social work and counselling
• Religion

2, 4, 7, 10, 13, 19, 21, 24

Information is your passion. You enjoy:
• Expressing yourself through writing, music, art.
• Doing experiments or researching a topic.
• Solving puzzles or problems.
• Studying or reading.

Jobs related to information are found in:
• Arts and entertainment
• Business and finance
• Scientific research
• Sales and services
• Tourism
• Law

Activity 4 ●

Creating Job Advertisements

1. Read the following list of jobs found on an Internet site.

Renovations and Restoration—Ready for a career that's a real fixer-upper?
Electrician—A power-full profession!
Fund-raiser—Make money collecting money.
Basketball Shoe Designer—Run faster. Jump higher. A career that's all about looking good.
Military Aircraft Technician—Become a Top Gun technician.

Park Ranger—Become a warden of the great outdoors.
Child Life Specialist—Make a child's visit to the hospital bearable.
Massage Therapist—The ultimate hands-on profession!
Animal Health Technologist—Extend a caring hand to our furry friends.

Optometrist—Feast your eyes on this career!

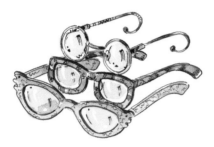

Pediatrician—Help kids get a healthy start.
Professional Sports Trainer—Keeps athletes ticking after they've taken a licking!
Overseas Red Cross Workers—Become a caring citizen of the world.
Criminologist—Make a career in crime pay if you're on the studious side.
Drama Teacher—Get into the act of this career!
Video Jockey—For those with star appeal and excellent communication abilities.
Jeweller—Discover a career that's a real treasure!

Bicycle Repair—How to kick-start a career!
Smoke-jumper—Join an elite crew of firefighters who protect our forests.
Freelance Writer—Creative writing as a career—fact or fiction?

Independent Performing Musician—Get the score on being a musical entrepreneur.
Biochemist—They find a cure for what ails you.
Forensic Scientist—Look for clues and uncover a fascinating career.
Golf Pro—The glamour is there—but the chances of making it are like a hole-in-one!

Information Technologist—All the bits and bytes you could ever want to play with.
Web Page Designer—The layout wizards of the Internet.
Maitre d'—Not just a fancy name for a waiter.
Comic Illustrator—A career in comic illustrating—more than just the Sunday funnies.
Dog Trainer—Who is training who?
Backhoe Operator—Get the digs on this career!
Home Inspector—Are you safe?

2. Select a job you are interested in from the list or from the Career Clusters chart on page 75 and create an advertisement with a "catchy" job description.

You might wish to file your advertisement in your portfolio.

Education and Job Choices

In Chapter 3, you set educational goals. Your level of education influences the types of job you can pursue. The following graph shows a variety of jobs or occupations organized by career cluster and levels of education and/or training. Note that you might have several jobs in your lifetime, but all in the same career, or field of interest. As you first learned in Chapter 4, Education and the Job Market, there are many more opportunities if you have a university degree, a college diploma, or apprenticeship training.

Education and Job Choices

Arts
Human Services
Technical
Business

- Graphic Artists
- Photographers' Assistants
- Special Effects Technicians
- Announcers
- Medical Technicians
- Dental Technicians
- Health Care Technicians
- Paralegals
- Social Services Workers
- Ministers

- Creative and Performing Artists
- Writers
- Librarians
- Probation Officers
- Psychologists
- Teachers
- Lawyers
- Pharmacists
- Veterinarians
- Dentists
- Doctors
- Computer Programmers
- Land Surveyors
- Architects
- Engineers
- Investors
- Counsellors
- Accountants
- Auditors

- Assembly Supervisors
- Process Operators
- Processing Supervisors
- Fishing Vessel Skippers
- Logging Machine Operators
- Underground Miners
- Forestry Supervisors
- Mapping Technicians
- Industrial Engineers
- Technical Inspectors
- Administrative Assistants
- Clerical Supervisors

- Health Services Assistants
- Assemblers
- Machine Operators
- Agriculture and Horticulture Workers
- Oil and Gas Drillers
- Logging and Forestry Workers
- Mine Service Workers
- Clerks
- Office Equipment Operators
- Distributors

- Food Counter Attendants
- Medical Assistants
- Labourers
- Primary Production Labourers
- Plant Labourers
- Cashiers

Education and/or Training Required

| **University** | **College, or apprenticeship, or two-years' training beyond high school** | **High school diploma, or some high school and on-the-job training** | **Some secondary school and some on-the-job training** |

Activity 5

Creating a Personal Venn Diagram

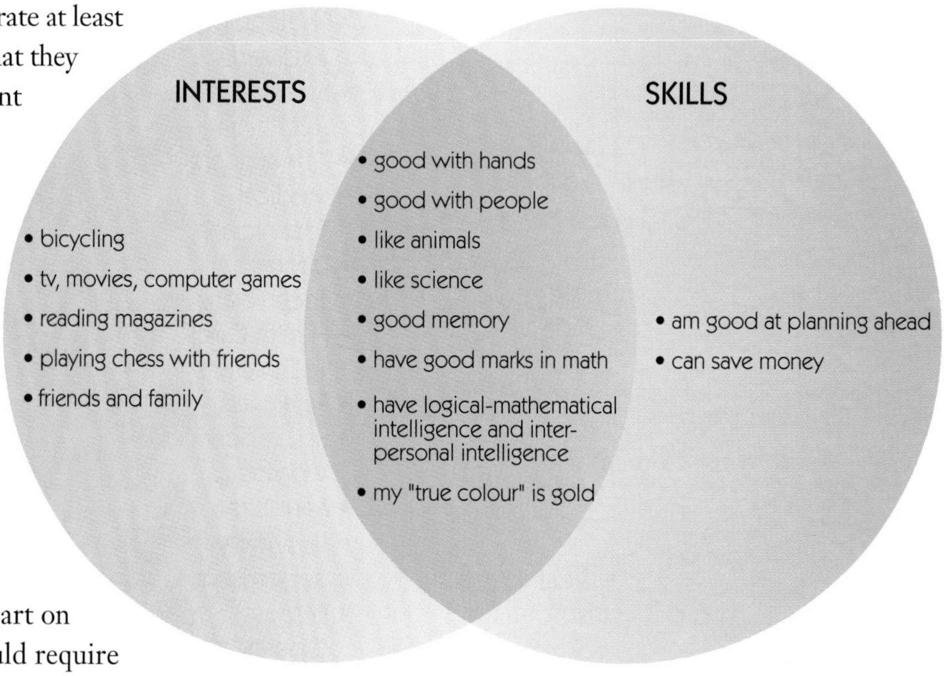

A Venn diagram is used to demonstrate at least two different subject areas to see what they have in common and what is different about the two. On a piece of paper, draw two overlapping circles. Label one circle "Interests" and the other circle "Skills." Using information you have gathered about yourself from activities in previous chapters, list your interests and skills in the appropriate circles. Write anything that is both an interest and a skill in the section where the circles overlap. See the sample Venn diagram at right.

Review the Career Clusters chart on page 75. Identify the jobs that would require the majority of characteristics listed in the central part of your Venn diagram. List these jobs underneath your diagram. You might wish to file your Venn diagram in your portfolio.

INTERESTS

- bicycling
- tv, movies, computer games
- reading magazines
- playing chess with friends
- friends and family

- good with hands
- good with people
- like animals
- like science
- good memory
- have good marks in math
- have logical-mathematical intelligence and inter-personal intelligence
- my "true colour" is gold

SKILLS

- am good at planning ahead
- can save money

PORTFOLIO

Creating a Family Tree of Careers

Talk to as many family members as you can about the career paths they have chosen. Ask each person to describe his or her employment history while you take notes. Ask your relatives about past generations. When you have gathered all the information, create a "Family Tree of Careers." A sample is included to get you started.

Do you notice any patterns in the jobs your family chose? Are the career choices you are interested in similar to those of your family? You might wish to share your family tree with the class and then file it in your portfolio.

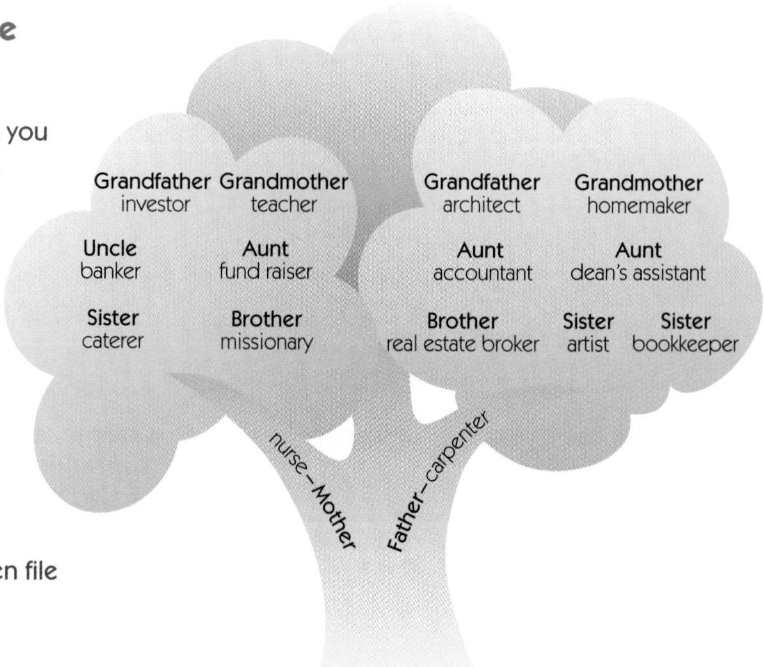

Grandfather investor **Grandmother** teacher **Grandfather** architect **Grandmother** homemaker

Uncle banker **Aunt** fund raiser **Aunt** accountant **Aunt** dean's assistant

Sister caterer **Brother** missionary **Brother** real estate broker **Sister** artist **Sister** bookkeeper

nurse~Mother Father~carpenter

Career Information Sources

As you begin to plan your future, it is important to have information about the choices that are available to you. There are many sources for gathering this information.

Guidance Offices: Your school guidance counsellor can provide you with career information.

Libraries: Use both your school and your community libraries. An excellent resource is the National Occupational Classification (NOC) book developed by the Canadian government.

Computers: There are numerous computer programs that provide career information. Some information software programs and the Internet are also good sources.

Career Centres: Your community and your board of education might have career centres.

Activity 6

Researching Careers

1. Form groups by choice of career cluster. Study the Career Clusters chart on page 75. List the jobs each member of your group is interested in or would like to know more about.

2. Brainstorm the kind of information you would like to have about the jobs and develop a set of questions. For example: How much education does it require? Is there a special school you have to attend? Do you need a licence to work? Do people work year-round or only at certain times of the year? What is the work environment like?

3. In pairs or individually, use a variety of the sources mentioned earlier to research your jobs. Find the answers to your set of questions and write a description of the jobs you researched.

   You might wish to file your research in your portfolio.

Copying Job Descriptions

Your class has researched many different types of jobs. Make copies of the job descriptions that interest you the most. Add them to your portfolio.

PROFILE

Alanis Morissette—Singer, Songwriter, and Performer

by Jeff Bateman

Born in Ottawa, Ontario, on June 1, 1974, Morissette's early studies included ballet, piano, and jazz dance. She was writing songs at the age of nine and released an independent single, "Fate Stay with Me," two years later that received modest national airplay. One of her program selections in high school was co-operative education in a music studio. She was a regular on the syndicated TV series *You Can't Do That on Television* before striking a creative partnership with Ottawa musician Leslie Howe from the recording group *One to One* (later *Sal's Birdland*).

After Morissette was signed to a publishing contract, Howe produced her major label debut, the dance-pop *Alanis* in 1991. "Too Hot" and "Feel Your Love" spurred the album to platinum in Canada, and Morissette won a Juno as Most Promising Female Vocalist. *Now Is the Time* was another high-energy dance album released in 1992.

Released from her record contract, Morissette relocated to Los Angeles and was signed in 1994 by Madonna's record company, Maverick. Her label debut in 1995, *Jagged Little Pill*, was a mature, compellingly frank collection of modern-rock originals produced and co-written by Glen Ballard. Led by the singles "You Oughta Know," "Hand in My Pocket," and "Ironic," the album sold in excess of 10 million copies in North America and Europe. It rapidly established Morissette as the intelligent and empowered

voice of a generation. She received four Grammy Awards in February 1996, the most Grammys ever won in a single year by a Canadian. She took home five Junos a few weeks later.

From *The Canadian Encyclopedia Plus,* © 1996 McClelland & Stewart Inc. Reprinted by permission.

1. List the different kinds of "smart" that Alanis possesses.

2. Do you agree with the statement "It rapidly established Morissette as the intelligent and empowered voice of a generation"? Why or why not?

3. Draw a time line depicting Alanis's career path.

Activity 7

Writing Biographies

In groups, brainstorm a list of famous people whose occupations appear in the Career Clusters chart. Each of you then select a few people to research. They might have careers to which you aspire, or be someone you admire. When the research is complete, write brief biographies of each person. You might wish to include photographs of the people with your biographies or an example of something they created, such as a book, a painting, or a software program. Meet in groups again, and present your biographies to one another.

In the Future

It is impossible to predict the future accurately. For example, futurists of the 1960s and 1970s foretold that there would be a greater use of computers. However, they did not foresee how computers would become an essential part of our lives and work. Still, it is possible to look at the facts today and imagine what could happen in the future. The following chart shows **trends**, or general directions, in Canadian society that are changing the workplace today and are creating new possibilities for tomorrow's workers.

TODAY'S FACTS	TOMORROW'S POSSIBILITIES
An aging population: The baby boomers are getting older. As a result, there will be more people in the 45-54 age group by the year 2000.	**More jobs for young people:** As the baby boomers age, many will retire. Since there aren't as many young people entering the work force as there are older people leaving, there will be more career opportunities for young people. **More job opportunities in services for older people:** An aging population will increase demand in areas such as health care, leisure activities, and educational services for older people.

More women in the work force: Women's participation in the work force is growing: many are mothers with children under 18 years of age.

More family-friendly workplaces: To ease the stress on working parents, more companies will allow flexibility in work schedules and family leave.

More jobs for people who provide services to working women: Child care workers, homemakers, house-cleaning services—there will be increasing demand for people who provide support services for families.

More education = better opportunities: Workers with good education and skills are getting jobs with good wages and career prospects. Workers with less education and skills are moving down the employment ladder in terms of wages, benefits, and prospects.

A more divided population: Canadian society could be divided into those who have wealth and those who don't. If unemployment remains high and the economy fails to generate a significant number of well-paying jobs, social problems may increase.

Growth of service jobs: Most new jobs today are in retail and wholesale business, financial and real estate services, entertainment, personal services, health, education, and social services, and transportation, communication, and utilities.

Continued demand for services: Increasingly, Canadians will turn to the service sector for employment. Business managers will seek out markets where they can supply products and services that are in demand.

New Ways to Work

Not only are new jobs being created all the time, but new ways of working are being created too. The 8-hour workday and 40-hour work week is becoming a thing of the past. For many reasons—personal lifestyle choices, availability, advancement of technology, and the cost of how work is done—flexibility concerning where and when people work is becoming more and more important for both employers and employees. Here are some new ways they are choosing to schedule their work time.

Telecommuting: Employees work at home, linked to the workplace by computers and fax machines.

Flex Time: Workers start and end their days on flexible schedules—for example, 7 a.m. to 3 p.m. instead of 9 to 5—within limits set by management.

Work Sharing: To avoid layoffs, an organization's work force might share the available work.

Job Sharing: Two people share the responsibilities, salary, and benefits of one full-time job.

Permanent Part-Time: The employee works fewer hours, but enjoys the same job security and benefits as a full-time employee.

Compressed Work Week: Employees work longer hours for fewer days.

Phased Retirement: This allows people to retire gradually by reducing their hours of work.

Leave Time: The employee may be absent from work without loss of employment rights for such options as family leave, maternity leave, educational leave, sabbatical leave, and personal leave.

The Impact of Technology

Another factor that impacts on career choice is the rapid growth of technology and how it affects jobs. Computers and other new technologies create new jobs, but also make others redundant. The Internet has connected businesses to the world, and information and knowledge have become important new products. Changing work styles, such as telecommuting and an increase in home-based, entrepreneurial businesses, have also affected people's lifestyles and needs. All of these factors make choosing a career that will carry you into the future an important decision.

© 1996 Washington Post Writers Group. Reprinted with permission.

IN THE NEWS

Lessons from the Future

by Frank Ogden

Imagine yourself back to the year 1905. You work for a company that manufactures buggy whips.

You learned leatherworking from your father, and your skills have guaranteed you steady employment since you were 14 years old. You don't worry about the future, because people will always need horses, buggies, and buggy whips.

Those new-fangled automobiles? They're expensive, unreliable, and dangerous—just a passing fad!

Technological Change Is Nothing New

Canadian workers today are in a situation similar to that faced by workers a hundred years ago. Technology has created hundreds of new products, making old ones obsolete.

Our economy is no longer fuelled by selling natural resources or mass manufactured products. More and more Canadians are working for industries that market ideas, information, and technology, including software developers, telecommunications companies, and businesses that develop and manufacture instruments such as robotics and computer controls.

The incredible advances in knowledge and technology are

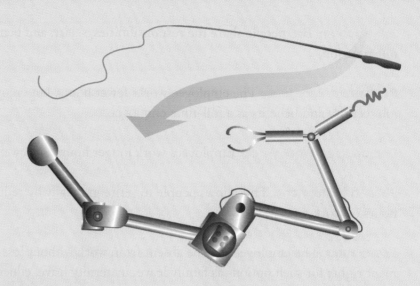

changing our work and lifestyles so completely that many people are calling the 1990s the dawn of the Information Age—a time when ideas and knowledge are the main forces in the development of new goods and services.

Jobs in the Future Will Be Constantly Changing

The leatherworker only knew one skill—how to work leather into buggy whips. If you're looking for a job in today's economy, you may have to add a few skills to those you already have.

Whatever kind of job you're looking for, chances are it now requires some computer skills. For example, if you want a secretarial job, you'll have to learn word-processing and electronic filing systems. If you're interested in shipping and warehousing, you're going to need to be familiar with computerized dispatch and inventory controls.

Acquiring these skills may mean some computer training and learning some basic math skills. It may mean sharpening your communications skills in reading and writing.

The most important skill, however, is one you probably already possess—the ability to be flexible and adaptable. Change in the Information Age is happening so quickly that no job will remain the same.

From Dr. Tomorrow's "Lessons from the Future." Reprinted by permission of Frank Ogden.

1. How might computer inventions, such as multimedia development and country-wide networks, affect our lives?

2. What do you think of an increasingly technological environment? Do you look forward to it or do you wish it would slow down? Do you look forward to the jobs it will result in?

Job Trends

The following lists forecast jobs that will be growing and declining in the future.

JOB GROWTH

- Technicians—computer, environmental, medical, automation, quality control
- All aspects of film and television production
- Food preparation—take-out, delis, home delivery
- Private school teachers
- Hospitality—adventure tours, luxury hotels
- Retailers—large discount stores, home office products
- Home renovators
- Farmers specializing in local markets
- Private security firms
- Massage and relaxation therapists
- Funeral directors
- Drivers for mail order or home shopping items
- Information technologists
- Paralegals
- Financial planners
- Marketing specialists
- Activation co-ordinators
- Registered nursing assistants/health care aids
- Software developers
- Engineers—electrical and mechanical

JOB REDUCTION

- Court reporters
- Legal secretaries
- Print journalists
- Doctors (except for those working with the elderly)
- Traditional farmers
- Bank tellers
- Inventory takers
- Printers (other than desktop)
- Department store and supermarket jobs
- Public school teachers

In the future, robots will replace workers in performing many routine functions, particularly where danger, accessibility, or great strength are factors.

Looking Back

1. Name three places where you can gather information about careers.

2. List two changes in today's society that will affect jobs in the future. Explain the effect they will have.

3. Do you agree with the lists on job growth and job decline? Are there some that you question? Make a list of the occupations that fall into these categories and the reasons why you picked them.

EXPLORATIONS

Reflections

What are your dreams for the future? Do you also have some worries or concerns about what is ahead? Reflect on what you think the future might hold for you.

Action!

Imagine that there is a psychic who is able to see the future by looking into a crystal ball. Several clients come to visit, asking questions about the future—careers, workplace trends, job opportunities, working in outer space, and so on. Role-play this scenario.

Goals

Based on the information you now have about future career possibilities and what your interests and abilities are, select the career that interests you the most. Make that your career goal. In order to achieve that goal, you will have to also set educational goals. Include educational goals for high school. Revisit the goals you chose for post-secondary education in Chapter 4. Do they need to be changed to meet your career goal? Create three action steps that will start you on the path to your future career.

Featuring. . .

Editorial: Write an editorial on the topic "The Changing Workplace."

Advertisement: Create an advertisement for an interesting job for today and for the future.

Advice Column: Respond to two readers who have written to the magazine asking for advice on how to choose a career that they will like.

Research: Conduct research on Canadian futurists and summarize what their predictions are for future workplace trends and job opportunities.

Personal Story/Interview: Interview someone you or your parents/guardians know whose job includes at least one of the "new ways to work" mentioned in this chapter. Find out how the change has affected his or her life. Prepare your interview for publication.

Setting Up Your Network

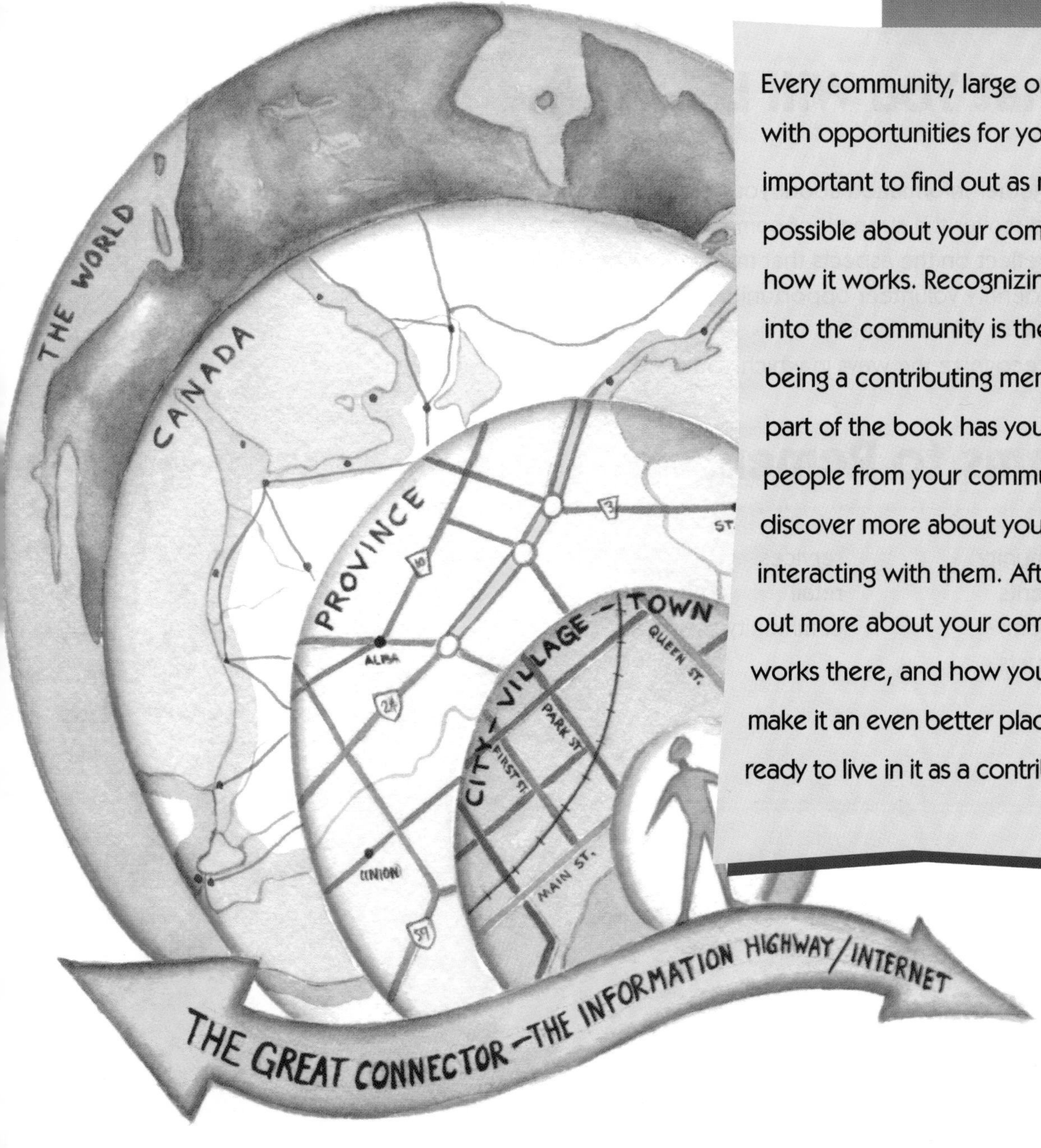

THE WORLD

CANADA

PROVINCE

ALPHA

UNION

CITY — VILLAGE — TOWN

QUEEN ST.

PARK ST.

FIRST ST.

MAIN ST.

THE GREAT CONNECTOR—THE INFORMATION HIGHWAY/INTERNET

Every community, large or small, is filled with opportunities for you. It is important to find out as much as possible about your community and how it works. Recognizing how you fit into the community is the first step to being a contributing member of it. This part of the book has you meet people from your community and discover more about yourself by interacting with them. After you find out more about your community, who works there, and how you can help to make it an even better place, you will be ready to live in it as a contributing member.

Resources in Your Community

What You Will Learn

- To gather information about your community.
- To discover the strength of community co-operation.
- To reflect on the aspects that make your community unique.
- To identify volunteer opportunities that interest you and will develop your skills for a future career.
- To recognize the ways in which you are a part of your community.

Terms to Remember

community   services
residents   retail
economy   community services
products

The dictionary defines a **community** as "a body of people living in the same place under the same laws." But is it not much more than that? People create the community, and it is what happens in it that makes it important to them. A community might have ten, a hundred, ten thousand, or a million people or **residents**. It might have a thousand buildings set very close together or fifty buildings set apart. It might have a few businesses or many. It might be built on a lake or it might have a river running through it. The streets might be straight and flat or twisted and hilly. Whatever the characteristics, it is still a community, and what happens in it depends on the people.

Businesses in Your Community

A community's **economy**—the management of material resources—is very important to its well-being. Consider the businesses that are necessary for people's day-to-day lives. What types of **products** are made locally? Visualize the stores on the main streets and throughout the area. What kinds of products are for sale? Think also about the **services** that must be provided to enable community homes and businesses to operate and the people to live comfortably. All of these factors contribute to the well-being of a community.

The Retail Community

The **retail** community consists of stores that sell, in small amounts, products such as groceries, hardware, clothing, and electronic equipment directly to the consumer. Most communities have retail stores that provide not only products, but also jobs.

Activity 1

What Stores Are in Your Community?

1. Make a list of products that your family generally needs to purchase in the stores where you live.

2. Create a chart, using the headings from the sample that follows, to show what stores are available in the area where you usually shop.

Stores in My Community

Name of Store	Type of Store	Estimated Number of Employees	Distance from My Home	Frequency of Use by My Family
SNAPS	Convenience	8	.25 km	daily
Bob's	Bakery	3	.25 km	daily
Loblaws	Supermarket	65	1 km	weekly
Your Hardware	Hardware	16	1 km	weekly
Planit	Building Centre	11	3 km	monthly
Greens'	Fruit/Vegtable	6	.25 km	weekly

When you have completed the chart for all the stores in your community, compare your results as a class.

- Which stores do all families use?
- Which ones do most families use?
- Which ones do only some families use?
- Are there products that are not available in your community? If so, how far must you go to get them?
- Do most families walk to the stores or get there by transportation?
- What stores have the most employees? The least employees?
- Which stores are used the most frequently?

CASE STUDY

Building Stronger Communities—a Success Story

A Community in Trouble

Port au Port, Newfoundland, sprawls across 96 kilometres of rugged coastline and includes 25 small towns with a population of about 8000. At one time, it was a thriving community with a successful local fishing industry and a limestone mine. There were a lot of jobs, including those generated by a nearby U.S. military base.

Then the bad times began. The military base closed, limestone no longer had a market, and the fishing industry hit rock bottom when an important fish-processing plant closed in 1987.

The changes hit Port au Port hard. The adults lived on seasonal work and unemployment benefits.

The drop-out rate at the high schools was between 60 and 70 percent.

A vicious cycle had begun. Young people routinely left school at 16 years old. Many girls became single mothers living on social assistance. Their children weren't doing well in school—possibly predicting future school failure and more drop-outs.

And people with potential were leaving. "I questioned the future of our rural community," says Mark Felix, of the Port au Port Economic Development Association. "I wondered where the leadership was going to come from in 30 years' time when most of our population [was] high school drop-outs and dependent on social programs."

Education Is Key

The residents of Port au Port decided they had to do something. And what they chose was to look at their community's education as a whole.

The community's call to action included people not normally involved in education. Members of social agencies and businesses joined school boards and residents to promote social change. "It was a new idea at the time," Felix points out, "but this agency co-operation turned out to be our greatest strength."

Calling themselves the Community Education Initiative, the group put several programs into place:
- Pre-kindergarten day-care to provide children with an enriched environment and parents with support programs.
- A variety of reading programs in the schools.
- Family Resource Centres within the schools, offering drop-in play programs, after-school programs, and family recreational events.
- The Pathfinder Learning Centre, providing other ways of learning for people who have dropped out of school and then returned to finish their education.

Port au Port also applied its teamwork approach outside the school system. Discussions with federal and provincial social agencies started other changes.

Developing an Economic Base

"We also want to develop an economic base in the community," says Beverley Kirby, the Co-ordinator of the Community Education Initiative. "And we want to nurture an educated population that can make the most of local opportunities." Port au Port is working to build on several areas of economic activity: tourism, aquaculture, and sheep farming.

The schools have developed careers in entrepreneurship, aquaculture, tourism, and agrifoods. "We're providing a lot of career awareness information," Kirby adds, "and not just to kids. We want to train parents to help their children make good career choices."

The Community Education Initiative has a number of successes under its belt. Teachers are reporting higher reading levels, the drop-out rate is decreasing, and more parents are actively involved with their children's education.

A student hard at work at the Pathfinder Learning Centre in Port au Port West, Newfoundland.

"Now we're working on helping high school students make the change to college or university," Kirby says. And the community has also started a series of televised town-hall meetings to discuss the future of Port au Port.

Interested in Helping Your Community?

What advice would Felix and Kirby give other struggling communities? "The main ingredient is people," Felix says. "You have to develop human resources, not infrastructure (the basic parts of a structure or system). You can always build infrastructure later. Kirby adds, "Focus on everyone working together to get things done."

Port au Port still faces an uphill battle, but its residents have taken action that will help keep young people in the community and create hope for the future.

Adapted from Canada Career Information Partnership, *Canada Prospects,* 1995/1996.

1. **The changes in Port au Port must have been a challenge for some people to accept. Write a few paragraphs from the point of view of a teenager, a woman, or an older man living in Port au Port. Include your reflections on how you felt about Port au Port before the changes, after the first meeting about the changes, and, finally, after the changes had begun and the town started to recover.**

Service Businesses

Many business opportunities in your community will be in the area of service. Who repairs a flat tire? Who do you call if a pipe bursts? Who provides fuel for heating systems? Who cuts people's hair? Where do people go for entertainment or a meal? Who provides access to television programs? These businesses are not always easy to see, but they are essential to the community.

What Services Are Available in Your Community?

Refer to the Yellow Pages in your telephone book and the advertisements in your community newspaper to get you started on this activity. Create a chart similar to the sample below.

Services in My Community

Name of Business	Service Offered	Estimated Number of Employees	Distance from My Home	Frequency of Use by My Family
Carpet Delight	Carpet Cleaning	3	2 km	1/year
Hair After	Hair Care	6	.5 km	1/month
Plumber Brothers	Plumbing	3	.5 km	as required
Keen Klean	Cleaners	3	.5 km	1/week

As a class, combine your findings and compare your results.
• What surprised you about the services available in the community?
• Which services are lacking?
• Which services are most numerous?
• Which services are used most?
• Which services employ the most people? The least?
• Which businesses interested you? Why?

Representing Your Community

Represent your community in one of the following ways.
• Create a soundscape by recording such sounds as vehicles, voices, construction, loud music, birds, rain, and wind.
• paint a mural.
• build a model.

Community Services

Community services are organizations that add to the quality of people's lives by providing services that promote health and well-being. They provide recreation and leisure activities as well as physical and mental health support-systems. Many of the services assist individuals and families; others interact with schools. The employees of community service organizations are people who like working with other people rather than with things. Many of them are volunteers from the community.

Activity

Identifying Volunteer Jobs

With your classmates, brainstorm a list of your community service organizations. Then refer to your local newspaper or telephone directory to see if there are any services to add to the list. Find out if the services use volunteers. Which volunteer activities appeal to you? What kind of skills would you develop if you volunteered in each? Which community service would help you develop skills for a future career? Record your findings on a chart like the following.

VOLUNTEER ACTIVITY	SKILLS PRACTISED
Serving in a Breakfast Program.	
Helping drivers deliver Meals on Wheels.	
Shelving books at a library.	
Copying, collating, and stapling.	
Answering the phone.	
Shovelling snow or mowing the lawn.	
Sorting and packing food at a food bank.	
Playing with preschoolers.	
Reading to seniors.	
Visiting seniors.	

 Contact the services in your community to discuss the work. Ask if there are any openings. Add the chart to your portfolio. You might include volunteering as one of your short-term goals.

IN THE NEWS

A Little Time Goes a Long Way

by Janice Turner

It's a glorious summer's day and Lisa Mak, 18, a high school graduate who's university bound, is serving a picnic lunch to a group of seniors. And she's smiling. Non-stop.

The night before, she'd spent three hours making assorted sandwiches and designing fruit trays. Before that, she'd picked up groceries for 17 guests—all members of Support Services for the Elderly.

"I've never shopped for so much food in my life!" says Lisa.

Mak and about 15 of her schoolmates raised the $100 for the food and drink by selling posters during the school year. They also received an $85 grant from the Bell United Way program—100 percent of what they asked for.

The program encourages youth aged 14 to 20 to come up with projects that will improve their communities. The funding comes from Bell Canada and is distributed through the United Way. The grant to Mak and her colleagues paid for door-to-door transportation to the park for all the guests.

"It's just marvellous," enthuses Olivia Berry, 74, relaxing after lunch in the bright, midday sun. "Without them, we wouldn't be out here today. We'd be sitting at home, and sitting at home does you no good. It's very nice that they've taken the time to be with us."

The group of teens has brought along a portable stereo for background music—a mix of pop and classical. Before and again after lunch some of the youngsters play bingo, chess, and checkers with their older friends. Others simply pair off and talk.

"When you help the community you feel good about yourself and the seniors don't feel so isolated," says Mak. "It helps them know what's going on through a teenager's perspective."

Eighty-something Ted Nielsen says the teens have demonstrated that they truly care. "They're beautiful, just terrific," he says. "With young people you have interesting things happening. It keeps you up to date."

Michael Follert, 16, notes that everyone will grow older, and no one should be forgotten. Besides, he thoroughly enjoys the company. "They've been young before and they understand what it's like. I do learn from them."

The students keep in touch with the seniors by phone, speaking to them once or twice

Lisa Mak and Olivia Berry enjoying themselves at a picnic sponsored by Support Services for the Elderly.

a week. The picnic is a chance for them to get together and celebrate.

Reprinted with permission—The Toronto Star Syndicate.

1. Discuss how each group (the volunteers and the Support Services for the Elderly participants) benefits from activities like this picnic.

2. Make a list of other activities that you think these picnic participants would enjoy.

3. These young people received a grant for this project to "improve their community." Discuss what kind of similar project you would like to do in your community.

Activity 5

Visiting the Community

As a class, identify two or three businesses or services in your community that interest you the most. Arrange to visit these sites and speak to a resource person, or have the resource people visit your classroom if you live in a rural area and cannot arrange transportation to the site. Before the meeting, prepare some questions and choose the students to ask them. Here are some categories and sample questions to get you started. Brainstorm to lengthen and strengthen the list.

Purpose of the workplace
- What product/service do you provide?
- Who buys/uses your product/service?
- How do you attract customers?

Scope of the workplace
- How many employees do you have?
- How many people use your product/service?
- How long has the business been in operation?

Employment profile
- What types of jobs are performed?
- What responsibilities do employees have?

Skills needed
- How did the employees learn to do their jobs?
- What skills will be needed in future employees?

Future trends
- How has this workplace changed?
- How will it change?
- How might increased technology affect your workplace?

Ideas for visits:
- Note the location of the site and its convenience for employees.
- Note the atmosphere of the place and the feelings you had there.
- Note the equipment and furnishings. Note the employees' behaviour, their clothing, their interaction.

After you have prepared a question sheet, use the following checklist to plan your visit.

Visiting the Community Checklist

☐ Pick a site to visit.

☐ Make an appointment to visit the site.

☐ Arrange transportation.

☐ Meet the resource person.

☐ Explore the site. (Look. Listen. Ask questions. Get involved.)

☐ Make notes about the visit with the help of your question sheet.

☐ Summarize your question sheet and write a report.

☐ Send a thank-you note.

☐ Discuss your reports with your class.

ADAM © Brian Bassett. Reprinted with permission of UNIVERSAL PRESS SYNDICATE. All rights reserved.

People Are the Key

While you have been studying your community, you have probably realized the strength of the people. Many of them might be people you know. Some might even be your relatives. As a class, start a list of the people who help to make your community a good place to live. Begin by listing the people who support your school, other than your teachers. Add to the list as you continue your study of communities.

Activity 6

Inviting Guest Speakers

Look through some copies of your local newspaper and clip articles about people in the community who interest you. Identify those you would like to have visit your class. You might need to contact the community's Chamber of Commerce, government offices, or the newspaper itself, or check the Yellow Pages, to find out how to get in touch with them. When you invite a speaker to the classroom, offer some guidelines about what is of interest to the class.

After each visit, fill out a report like the sample that follows, especially if the speaker's career, business, or volunteer activity is one that interests you for the future. File it in your portfolio.

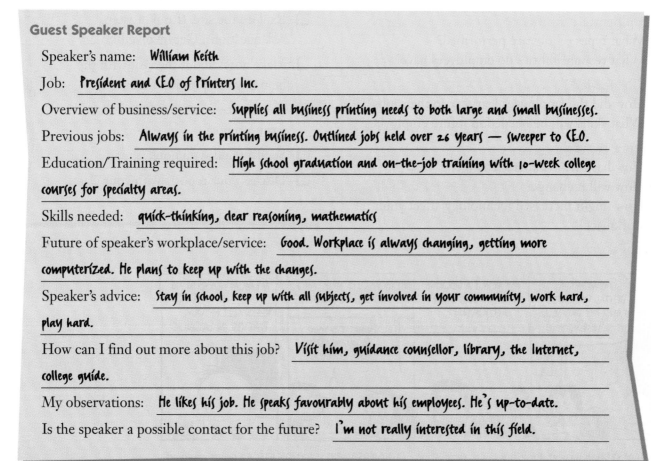

Guest Speaker Report

Speaker's name: **William Keith**

Job: **President and CEO of Printers Inc.**

Overview of business/service: **Supplies all business printing needs to both large and small businesses.**

Previous jobs: **Always in the printing business. Outlined jobs held over 26 years — sweeper to CEO.**

Education/Training required: **High school graduation and on-the-job training with 10-week college courses for specialty areas.**

Skills needed: **quick-thinking, clear reasoning, mathematics**

Future of speaker's workplace/service: **Good. Workplace is always changing, getting more computerized. He plans to keep up with the changes.**

Speaker's advice: **Stay in school, keep up with all subjects, get involved in your community, work hard, play hard.**

How can I find out more about this job? **Visit him, guidance counsellor, library, the Internet, college guide.**

My observations: **He likes his job. He speaks favourably about his employees. He's up-to-date.**

Is the speaker a possible contact for the future? **I'm not really interested in this field.**

PROFILE

Helping the Homeless

by Scott Steele

From 1989 to 1994 Ken Lyotier, the self-described 49-year-old alcoholic and "full-time dumpster-diver," combed the alleyways and garbage bins of downtown Vancouver—which has no blue-box recycling program in high-density buildings—for bottles and cans he could return to local retailers. The problem was, there were limits on how many each would accept. Lyotier and other street people in the city's downtown Eastside—the neighbourhood with the lowest per capita income in Canada—decided to begin a grassroots recycling initiative. Predicting that they could gather five million bottles and cans a year at a central location, pay cash to the collectors, and then return the containers to manufacturers for a deposit and a small handling fee, they approached VanCity Community Foundation. The foundation agreed to give them an interest-free loan of $12 500—and extended a further $12 500 line of credit, personally guaranteed by an anonymous VanCity member. In 1995, United We Can opened in a storefront on Vancouver's East Cordova Street.

According to the soft-spoken Lyotier, now general manager of the facility, which employs four full-time sorters and four part-timers, up to 400 people a day bring in bottles and cans for cash. Hauling their spoils in shopping carts and green garbage bags, many are homeless, have problems with substance abuse, or suffer from mental illness.

In just 18 months, United We Can has not only met its commitments to VanCity, but has also paid out $600 000 in cash to the collectors—and has provided a much-needed environmental service.

Maclean's, July 1, 1996. Reprinted with permission.

Frank Lyotier turned bottle and can collecting into a recyling business for the homeless.

1. **Create a poster that Ken Lyotier can post around Eastside that tells people how they can get involved in the United We Can project as a collector or as a supplier of bottles and cans.**

2. **What two questions would you like to ask Ken Lyotier about his involvement in United We Can?**

3. **What two questions would you like to ask one of the people who bring in bottles and cans each day?**

4. **"People are the key" is a phrase used earlier in this chapter. Frank Lyotier and his supporters are the key to the success of an initiative that helps hundreds of people while improving the environment. Create a plaque to be presented by the City of Vancouver to United We Can.**

Activity 7

Creating an Information Kit

Imagine that a furniture refinisher is thinking of moving a small business into the community where you live. He is married and has two children. For his workshop, he will need a location that is close to transportation. He plans to hire four employees.

Work with a small group to plan an information kit for this family. What facts will they need to know about your community before they can make up their minds? What aspects of the community will they find suitable and appealing?

Activity 8

Webbing Your School Community

Create a list of the characteristics of a community. Then think of your school as a community. Which characteristics are the same? What people come into the school every day? Who works so that you can learn? Think of all the jobs that make it possible for you to attend school. Make a list and then create a web diagram to represent your school community. Include the people's names beside their role.

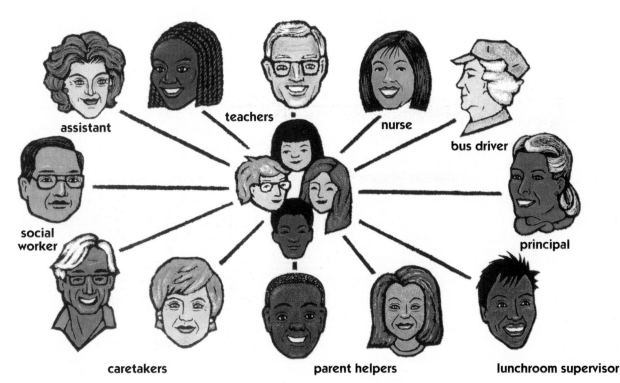

Activity 9

Creating a Welcome Package

1. Imagine that visitors from another province are coming to your school. Put together a Welcome Package for them. Include a map of the school, historical information about it, an outline of who is there on a daily basis, and the activities that help to make it a community. If possible, include an interview with a student or an employee of your school. Ask the person in what ways he or she feels the school is a community. You might also want to include a calendar of special events for the year.

2. Repeat the activity above for new students. Add items of interest to them, such as How to Get Involved in Your New School Community.

How Will You Fit into the Community?

Now that you are familiar with the characteristics of a community and all the people and services that work together to make communities successful, visualize the part that you will play in a community in the future. What will be your responsibilities as a community member?

With your classmates, paint a mural depicting how you see your roles in a future community.

Or

Create a mock radio or television program, in which you interview classmates about how they see their roles in a future community.

J O U R N A L

Reflecting on Choices

Reflect on the mural or interview that you and your classmates created. What surprised you about your classmates' choices? What were the reasons behind your contribution to the mural or interview? Record your observations in your journal.

Looking Back

1. In your opinion, what are the important parts of a community?

2. Define the word *economy* and describe why it is important to a community's well-being.

3. Name three service businesses that have characteristics in common.

4. Describe three different types of community services in your area.

EXPLORATIONS

Reflections

Write the name of your community vertically on the page. Beside each letter, write a sentence, word, or phrase that expresses how you feel about your community.

Goals

Look back at the educational goals that you have set for yourself. How do they fit with some of the jobs in your community that you found out about in this chapter? Which of these jobs now interest you? Try to find out more about them. Add any information you obtain to your portfolio.

Action!

Have one or two students copy the following situations on individual pieces of paper, place them in a box, and mix them up. Form pairs or threes, and have one of your group members pull out a piece of paper. Create a short skit based on the situation to illustrate what a new student encounters on his or her first day at school.

- Guidance interview to get timetable
- Information session on school rules
- Changing classes
- Lunch time
- Gym class
- Language Arts class
- Bus trip to new home
- First evening
- Three months later

Featuring. . .

Editorial: Write a letter to the editor either to complain about the lack of community services in your area or to praise the work of one of the community services in your area.

Advice Column: Write a response to the following letter.

> Dear Andy,
> I hope that you can help me. We are getting ready to move to a new town. I am looking forward to it, but feel very nervous about going to a new school where I do not know anyone. Please give me some advice on how to adjust to my new situation.
>
> Thanks in advance,
> Roy, 17 years old

Personal Story/Interview: Interview a person who volunteers in your school. Write a story that outlines the person's previous relevant experience, describes the type of volunteer work done in the school, and expresses the volunteer's reasons for involvement. Add a photo if possible.

Research: Speak to a real estate salesperson in your community about local sales statistics on a yearly basis. Compare yearly sales for a five-year period. What trends can you see? Ask the school secretary for statistics of how many students move away and how many move in by year. What comparisons can you make?

Advertisement: Create a radio script for an advertisement that will attract new families to your community. Include local attractions, businesses, and services that will be of interest to newcomers.

Examining Role Models

What You Will Learn

- To identify characteristics of positive role models.
- To select possible role models for your future.
- To explore how role models in the media influence young people's career choices.

Terms to Remember

role model
characteristics

A **role model** is a person whose part played in life is especially worth copying or imitating. Role models can have a big influence on the lives of many people, in many different ways. What characteristics make a worthy role model? What choices have they made and what actions have they taken that make them outstanding individuals? This chapter offers profiles of people who are role models for others. As you read about them, you can think about your own role models. You can determine what you can do to become the person you want to be.

What Is a Role Model?

Think of a person you admire. It could be someone famous in his or her field of work, someone in the community, or someone in your family. What special **characteristics** or qualities does that person have that make him or her admirable? What do you like about how that person acts and what he or she does? The following chart lists some characteristics and resulting actions that most people would find worthy.

CHARACTERISTIC	ACTION
Aware of the needs of others	Works as a volunteer
Resourceful	Creates new clothes from old ones
Reliable	Never breaks promises
Optimistic	Can find something positive in every situation
Brave	Stands up for people's rights

Activity 1

Identifying Characteristics

Think of other admirable characteristics to add to the chart and give examples of actions that illustrate them. Record the results so they can be shared with the class and referred to in future activities.

CASE STUDY

Inspired Connections

by Sharon Doyle Driedger

Dr. Arlette Lefebvre's voice falters, remembering her first encounter with a young patient named Laura. The Grade 3 student had contracted meningitis and—to save her life—doctors had to amputate her legs. "She was a figure skater," says Lefebvre, a psychiatrist at Toronto's Hospital for Sick Children where Laura was treated. "She woke up without legs—she was depressed, she didn't want to live, she didn't want to eat. I thought, 'How can I give this kid hope that there is life without legs?'" To help Laura deal with her loss, Lefebvre hooked her up to Ability OnLine, an innovative electronic support group she had established a year earlier. "One good role model is worth a thousand psychiatrists," Lefebvre contends. "I put her in touch by computer with Carlos Costa, a wonderful swimmer without legs. Now, she is Rollerblading with her prosthetic legs."

Ability OnLine—the first service of its kind in Canada—handles about 1200 calls a day across Canada, the United States, Europe, and Australia. The free e-mail link allows chronically ill, disfigured, or disabled young people to communicate from their homes or hospital beds with others who have a disability, as well as with friends, family, classmates, and volunteer mentors. "We've just had our millionth call," says Lefebvre, who started the program six years ago with a single computer.

In 1992, she realized her plan for a "friendly on-line environment" with the help of Brian

Dr. Arlette Lefebvre and some of the young people she's helped with Ability OnLine.

Hillis, a retired firefighter and computer wizard, volunteers, and donations from private sources. Ability OnLine now has more than 5000 current users, but Lefebvre is determined to expand. "My dream is to have a laptop in every [hospital] room," she says.

Lefebvre spends five hours every evening answering young people's e-mail messages. "Putting people in touch with each other," she says, "is my main goal." With Ability OnLine, Dr. Lefebvre found a way to do just that.

Maclean's, July 1, 1996. Reprinted with permission.

1. Make a list of words that you think best describe Arlette Lefebvre. Which of these characteristics do you admire the most? Add them to your chart, if you have not already included them.

2. How do Lefebvre's characteristics suit the career she has chosen? What other jobs do you think she would do well, and why?

Identifying Your Positive Qualities

What you do shows people who you are. Think about yourself in a variety of situations with people from different age groups. Some sample situations are:

• Visiting your grandmother in a seniors' residence.
• Attending a large family celebration or reunion.
• Going to a younger brother's or sister's baseball game.
• Going to a sporting event.
• Participating in a school play production.

Which of your character traits come to mind when you picture yourself in these situations or others that you think of? Record the situation and the character traits in your journal.

Activity ②

Identifying Role Models

1. With your classmates, make a list of people who are positive role models. They can be people in your family, people in the community, or famous people in any professional field.

2. Work independently to list the qualities each of these role models has that make him or her admirable and the actions that demonstrate these qualities.

3. Share your findings as a class.
   • Which role models are most popular with your peers?
   • What characteristics do many of the role models have in common?

FOR BETTER OR FOR WORSE © Lynn Johnston Prod., Inc. Reprinted with permission of UNIVERSAL PRESS SYNDICATE. All rights reserved.

IN THE NEWS

Raptors Phenomenon Can Relate to Boys and Girls Mission

by Michael Clarkson

At a recent Toronto Raptors practice at Glendon College, young students from a Toronto school had their noses pressed up against the gymnasium window, wide-eyed at the sight of their hero on the court inside—Damon Stoudamire. They knew they weren't allowed into the gym, but Stoudamire motioned to them. "Hey, kids, c'mon in," he smiled. And about 25 children rushed in and sat on the floor to watch the NBA's rookie of the year take foul shots—to the embarrassment of team officials.

An hour before a recent exhibition game at SkyDome, Stoudamire emerged to have a courtside photograph taken with four nervous youngsters from the West Scarborough Boys and Girls Club. It wasn't the best of days for him. The young Raptor would have to sit out that night's game with a charley horse injury. But he bounded over to the youngsters to introduce himself, signed autographs, and made them feel at ease as the photographer went about his work.

Stoudamire's new stardom in the National Basketball Association hasn't distanced himself from young fans. He knows about accessibility and role models and the need for children to

Raptors' Damon Stoudamire with members of the West Scarborough Boys and Girls Club.

have motivation and structure. That's one reason there's a scholarship in his name for members and volunteers of the Boys and Girls Clubs of Ontario. Another reason is, Stoudamire grew up in such a grassroots program in his hometown of Portland, Oregon.

"I went to a community centre every day after school, Monday through Saturday," he recalled. "I played hoops and ping-pong and bumper pool. It's important for kids to have an outlet, to keep them out of trouble."

There are 24 Boys and Girls Clubs in Ontario. Many of their members, like Stoudamire himself, are from single-parent families. Others are latch-key kids who stop in for games and friendship after school. Many are from low-income families.

"Damon is an absolutely excellent role model," says

Marion Price, Ontario executive director of the clubs. "Our slogan is Every Kid Has Potential. Damon grew up in a setting like our kids face, and look what he has become. He knows where he came from and where he's going to."

The Toronto Raptors Foundation (the team's charity arm) has donated $20 000 for the scholarships, which will go to 14 people who have been members or volunteers at the Boys and Girls Clubs for at least three years. Most of the winners joined their neighbourhood club at an early age, spent formative years there, and now that they're older and pointed in a positive direction, give hours back to the club as volunteers. Their scholarship money will go towards tuition at a college or university. "These students wouldn't normally make it to post-secondary school if they didn't get a scholarship," Price said. The Raptors have also helped fund youth programs at Boys and Girls Clubs across Canada.

Stoudamire is thankful he had such community clubs to go to as a boy, as he developed his basketball skills to the point he was able to win a scholarship to the University of Arizona. His mother, Liz Washington, had to work as an accounting clerk at a trucking company after his father, Willie, left home when Damon was young. Since then, Willie has come back into his life and now acts as one of his agents. In his senior year, Stoudamire was drafted seventh overall in 1995 by the Raptors. As the engine for the expansion team's offence, he beat out other high-profile players to win the coveted rookie of the year honours. Stoudamire's quickness and fierce desire helped Toronto become competitive in its first year in the NBA.

Reprinted with permission — The Toronto Star Syndicate.

⸱⸱⸱

Setting a Fine Example for Native Youth

by Janice Turner

Strong family support and an Olympic champion for inspiration gave Sara Beaudry enough confidence and determination to "stay on the right path." She took up cross-country running, completed high school, and is proudly raising a son on her own. In 1990, she earned a gold, silver, and two bronze medals in track and field at the North American Indigenous Games. Three years later, the team she coached at the games brought home 14 medals. And just last year, she won herself another silver.

Today, the 24-year-old Ojibway volunteers with the National Native Role Model Program in hopes of making a difference in the lives of Native youngsters. The program dates back to the 1984 summer Olympics in Los Angeles when Beaudry's hero, Quebec Mohawk Alwyn Morris, won gold and bronze medals for Canada in kayaking. After winning the gold, he held up an eagle feather—the symbol of honour, friendship, and life—as a gesture to all North American Native people. A year later, he received the Order of Canada.

The program focusses on education, motivation, and positive reinforcement, and encourages Native American youth to realize their potential by taking control of their lives. It is federally funded, Native designed and operated, and rooted in the tradition of the seven sacred gifts: wisdom, love, respect, bravery, honesty, humility, and truth.

Beaudry and Morris have met five times during the past ten years. "I've been in total awe of him," says Beaudry, who named her son after her personal role model. "I know first-hand the impact that a role model can have on one's life," she says. "He inspired me to be the best I could be. He challenged me to make a difference and to believe

Sara Beaudry (left) and friend.

in myself and my dreams. The circle is complete as I am now the role model."

Beaudry was appointed to the two-year position with the role model program in February [1996] and has already visited with more than 15 Native American youth groups, most of them on reserves. She continues to run several times a week. "I think the strongest message I can send out is that my running has helped me stay on the right path," she says. "It's given me something to focus on and helped me to lead a healthy lifestyle."

The youngest of ten children, Beaudry spent most of her youth in Sudbury. In May, she moved to the Wikwemikong reserve on Manitoulin Island with her five-year-old son Alwyn to join the rest of her extended family. Beaudry is currently recreation co-ordinator for the reserve's youth centre.

"I try to get my message across by talking about my life and I haven't had any easy life raising a son by myself," she says. She separated from his father before their child was born. It also wasn't easy being the only Native American student at her Sudbury school. "I was teased," she recalls.

When speaking to kids, Beaudry then turns to the positive things in her life—her family and her commitment to physical health and her determination to stay in school. "I try to make them (Native American youths) understand that there's more out there than drugs and alcohol. There's their education and their culture. I know sometimes I'm getting through to them." She encourages young people to be active in their communities and to organize local youth councils.

"I want them to take responsibility for who they are and to try to build a future for themselves," she says. "I just try to encourage them to not listen to what other people have to say about who we are and where we come from. If you listen to that and believe it, it's just going to bring you down."

Reprinted with permission—The Toronto Star Syndicate.

PORTFOLIO

Describing a Role Model

Write a description of a role model who interests you. Include such details as personal traits and life events that shaped the person's character, education, and job history. You might need to research the information or, if your role model is someone who lives in the community, you might be able to interview him or her.

Or

Mount a picture of a role model on a background that represents something about that person's job; for example, an artist on a painter's palette, a musician on a lyric page, a computer programmer on a printout. Include a few important facts about the person on your display.

File your description in your portfolio.

PROFILES

Mary Simon

by Brian Bergman

For a brief moment, Mary Simon is savouring the comforts of home—in her case, a two-storey wood-frame house in central Ottawa. The bookshelves are filled with volumes on northern Canada, and soapstone carvings, prints, and paintings by northern artists adorn nearly every centimetre of display space. Just back from a five-day trip to Norway, Simon has only a few days to unwind before embarking on a ten-day journey to Greenland and Russia. It is all part of her job as Canada's ambassador for circumpolar affairs and chairperson of the newly formed Arctic Council, an eight-nation organization that is designed to foster co-operation in the northernmost regions of the planet. It also means spending more than half of each year on the road—a wanderer's existence that is nothing new to the Inuit leader. "I seem to have been travelling all my life," she says with a hearty laugh.

Born in Kangirsualujuak (George River) in northern Quebec, Simon spent much of her first 15 years moving with her family from camp to camp by dog team or canoe. Her Manitoba-born father, Bob May, who is white, went north as a Hudson Bay manager. He stayed on to found a fly-in fishing and hunting business and to marry Simon's mother, Nancy, who is Inuk. The second eldest of eight children, Simon says she learned early on about "living close to the land" and how to sew her own parkas, and *kamiks*, or traditional boots made of caribou, walrus, or seal hide. The family spoke Inuktitut and Simon took much of her schooling through correspondence courses. She credits those years with giving her a firm

Mary Simon, Canada's ambassador for circumpolar affairs and chairperson of the Arctic Council.

grounding in two very different cultures. "I can live down here in a house like this," she says with a sweep of her hand, "or I can go north and live in a tent. I'm comfortable either way."

Good thing, too. These days, Simon's life is punctuated by cellular phone calls, faxes, and complicated plane schedules. Since 1994, when she became the first Inuit ambassador in Canada, Simon has worked tirelessly to help found the Arctic Council, which held its first meeting in Ottawa this September [1996]. Her goal, she says, is to show that international co-operation can have results—preserving, for example, the Arctic environment and creating northern jobs through free trade in northern products.

For Simon, the Arctic Council is the culmination of a career that has seen her play a leading role in several Inuit institutions. But it required some sacrifices. For most of her adult years, Simon has had to make her home base far from northern Quebec, where her parents and siblings still live. Before pulling out pictures of herself and the fish she caught during a recent visit home, Simon remarks sadly, "The hardest part of my job is being away from my family so much." She has also had to adjust to life in urban Canada, where the casual friendliness of a Northerner is sometimes viewed with suspicion, if not outright alarm. "At first," she recalls with a smile, "I'd say hello to strangers and make eye contact. People would look at me like I was crazy."

To relax, Simon and her husband, former CBC broadcaster Whit Fraser, canoe, camp, and ski at every opportunity. She also cherishes her time with her three grown children, from a previous marriage, and the four grandchildren that they have given her. As her long-distance duties beckon, those moments seem increasingly precious.

Maclean's, December 23, 1996. Reprinted with permission.

Dean Lee: The Original Boy Wonder

by Karishma Gabriel

Look up in the sky! It's a bird, it's a plane! No! It's Dean Lee! Who is he? As a volunteer with the Boys and Girls Club in Dartmouth, Nova Scotia, and Chairperson of the National Youth Council, Dean Lee is truly a superhero to the kids and adults he encounters each day.

Dean's long association with the club began when he was a three-year-old in the preschool program. He was hooked and became a regular member, than later a youth volunteer at the Club. "He's been a member since he was three and has developed into a fine young man. He's a good student, likes sports, and holds down a part-time job. He's a well-rounded kid with a beautiful personality," says Roy Adair, Executive Director of the Dartmouth Boys and Girls Club.

"As an only child, the club gave me the chance to make friends. It's a real friendly environment. When I'm not at home or in school, I'm at the club. It's like my second home," says Dean.

Dean was raised by his mom, who had a "very positive influence" on him and who instilled in her son the values of discipline and hard work. "She always encouraged me to keep going and not give up, to stay positive and overcome any barriers."

Dean is also Chairman of the National Youth Council, the brainchild of the Boys and Girls Clubs of Canada. The NYC strives to give "equal representation to youth" across the country. "The NYC believes in the process of youth empowerment and are committed to providing a voice to be heard on a national level," Dean explained. The Council's aim is to ensure that young people are involved in contemporary political and social issues affecting youth.

Dean was picked as the 1995 poster boy for the United Way. His biggest thrill is being a role model for kids. "I'm noticed whenever I go out. Little kids tell me they want to have their picture up, too. And I just tell them, keep reaching for the top and maybe one day you'll be someone else's role model."

Dean credits his mom, the club, and the NYC for his growth and development. The 18-year-old is presently at Dartmouth High School and is looking to pursue a bachelor of arts in sociology and psychology and eventually a masters in education and social work. Ultimately, Dean wants to "give back" to the community that has given him so much. "Even if I go away to study, in the States or in Ontario, I'll come back to Dartmouth and the Boys and Girls Club because they really helped me out."

So who is Dean Lee? He's motivated, active, intelligent, a positive role model, and just a really nice guy! Look for Dean Lee action figures, coming soon to a store near you!

Reprinted from *TG Magazine*, www.tgmag.ca

Bruce Craig

by Victor Dwyer

He is a teacher whose lessons have touched almost everyone in tiny Cypress River, Manitoba. "Bruce Craig sees the world through his students' eyes, and teaches them to believe that what they want to do, they can do," says Marianne Anderson, whose three sons have all attended Cypress River Elementary School, where Craig is principal, physical education instructor, and teacher of Grades 4, 5, and 6. His fellow teachers agree. "He can get those kids to do amazing things," says Irene Plaetinck. "With him, teaching means making every single student shine."

In fact, ever since Craig moved to the Cypress River area after graduating from the University of Manitoba in 1977, the lessons have been piling up. And so, last April, the 200 citizens of the farming community decided to teach Craig, 43, a lesson of their own. Theirs would be a lesson in gratitude. Together, they produced a six-page, single-spaced, typewritten nomination outlining in detail why Craig should win the first annual Lieutenant-Governor of Manitoba Elementary School Classroom Teacher Award.

"When I heard what they were up to, I asked them not to do it," recalls Craig. "There are so many teachers out there with bigger mountains to climb." But the parents of Cypress River would have none of it, and set to work chronicling his story. It includes tales of a man who acts out the water cycle by jumping on and off his desktop, who gives up his lunch hours to offer private harmonica lessons, and who teaches in costume on special occasions.

In June, Craig found himself at the official residence of Lieutenant-Governor Yvon Dumont. Before a crowd that included Craig's wife, three children, and parents, Dumont announced that Craig was the unanimous first choice of a province-wide jury of parents and school trustees.

A visit to his modest, brown-brick schoolhouse, where students are invited to take a hands-on approach to learning, makes it easy to understand

Bruce Craig, the ideal elementary teacher.

why. One recent example: a month-long project on dinosaurs, for which Craig brought three electric drills to class and alternated lessons with ear-splitting workshops in which students recreated dinosaur skeletons from livestock bones. "Not every child is great at Math or Writing," explains Craig. "I'm always looking for a place in every lesson where all my students can marvel at their own unique strengths."

If one lesson informs all the others Craig teaches, it is that there is always a place for wonder and possibility. Pausing during a discussion on the solar system last month, Craig stood before his students, his eyes suddenly as wide as saucers. "How many of you believe there is life on other planets?" whispered the teacher. As a roomful of hands slowly made their way skyward, Craig's shot up above the others. "I sure do," he said. "Why not?" Why not indeed.

Maclean's, December 23, 1996. Reprinted with permission.

1. The role models about whom you have read have made important choices about who they are and where they want to be. Discuss the challenges they faced, and what they might have given up to pursue their dreams.

2. For each of the role models, identify the benefits they have gained from their experiences.

Learning from Role Models

Many people attribute their success to a famous person they admired when they were young. That role model might have been a movie star, an inventor, a surgeon, or an athlete. They probably never spoke to that person, and yet he or she set a worthy example to follow.

People in the media also trigger the popularity of certain occupations. For example, there was an increase in the number of students who chose computer careers after the success of Bill Gates, who developed MS-DOS and founded Microsoft®. Every four years, the Olympics renews people's interest in sports careers. The "overnight successes" of performers like Alanis Morissette might spur individuals on to becoming singers. Because of the exposure, or extensive coverage, that people receive in the media, their actions have a strong impact on young people and the careers they choose for themselves.

Comparing Professionals

With a partner, pick a career that would be highly visible in the media; for example, politician, model, athlete, medical researcher, musician, or lawyer. Review back copies of newspapers and magazines at the library to find as many articles as you can on people in that profession. Identify the individuals who are receiving the most media attention. Record any personal attributes and actions that are mentioned in the articles. Then outline why that person would or would not make a good role model for young people. Report your findings to the class.

Making Choices

In your journal, write an entry about education and career choices that you might make in the future and how they will affect your life as an adult.

Visualizing What You Would Say

If you could spend ten minutes talking to a person you admire, what would you say? Would you explain why you admire him or her? Would you ask who he or she admired as a young person? Would you get an autograph? Would you ask about something specific he or she did? Write your reflections on a sheet of paper, or create a song about the experience, or draw a storyboard about the incident. File it in your portfolio.

Looking Back

1. When you think back on the characteristics of the role models you have read about, met, and/or discussed, what are some of the personal characteristics they have that you would like to have?

2. Name three people who could be your role models and explain why you chose them.

3. Describe how the lifestyles of your role models meet your expectations of your future lifestyle.

EXPLORATIONS

Reflections

Imagine yourself as a role model for the next generation of students. Describe what personal characteristics you will have, how you will spend your time, what job you will be performing, how you will be dressed, what your work environment will be like, with whom you will be interacting . . . and anything else that will complete the picture. Allow yourself to dream of all the possibilities!

Goals

The role models profiled in this chapter had, and continue to have, a focus for their future. List three goals you have for your future.

Action!

You are a successful vice-president who has worked up from "the bottom" of a construction company, where you started as a labourer. With three other students in your class, role-play a scene in which you tell your family (partner and children) that you want to give up your office job and return to physical labour.

Featuring. . .

Editorial: Write an editorial about the importance of positive television role models for young people.

Advice Column: Write a letter to a student who thinks his or her friend is being overly influenced by a negative role model.

Personal Story/Interview: Write a personal story about a peer whom you consider to be a good role model.

Advertisement: Ask each person in your class for a picture and/or a description of one of his or her role models. Create a full-page advertisement with these items and the headline "Thanks for the Inspiration."

Research: Look at books in the biography and autobiography sections of the library. Skim through them to see who people identify as the person(s) who affected them most. Share this task with other students so you can get enough samples to look for trends.

Looking for Mentors

What You Will Learn

- To identify people in your life who are mentors to you and to others.
- To identify young people whom you have mentored and whom you could mentor in the future.
- To learn about the type of mentor you want and how to find one.

Terms to Remember

mentor
mentoring
correspond

A **mentor** is a trusted counsellor or guide. Many adults remember a person who played a special role in their personal development. That person, often older, gave support not available from peers or family members. He or she might have provided inspiration, information, career guidance, and exposure to new activities and ideas. You also might have had mentors in your life without even realizing it. In this chapter, you will identify past mentors in your personal life, find new ones to help you, and learn how to become a mentor yourself.

PORTFOLIO

Identifying Past Mentors

Identify people in your life who have been mentors, or who have guided and encouraged you along the way. They might be people in your family, at school, or in the community. In a web like the one here, write their names and describe what they did to help you (action).

Mentors in My Life

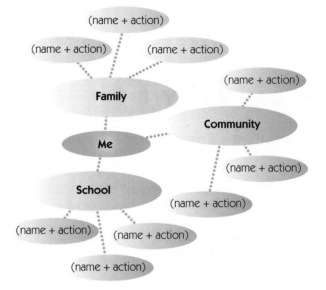

(name + action)

(name + action)   (name + action)

(name + action)

Family

Community

Me

(name + action)

School

(name + action)

(name + action)   (name + action)

(name + action)

Being a Mentor

In the past, you might have been a mentor without even realizing it. Have you:
- Been a reading buddy to a younger student in your school?
- Coached another student in a sport in which you were both interested?
- Helped someone learn to play a musical instrument?
- Shared your hobby with someone?
- Participated in a lunch monitor program?
- Made sure that a younger neighbour reached home safely each day?

If you have done any of these things, you have been a mentor. **Mentoring** is a relationship in which one person has a skill, knowledge, or support to give to another person.

Reflecting on Your Mentoring Experience

Think back to a time when you have been a mentor to someone.

• In what ways did you help?

• Did you do it more than once?

• How did you feel?

• What did the other person do or say to show he or she enjoyed being with you?

Describe your experiences in your journal.

Activity  1

Presenting Your Mentoring Abilities

1. Set up an information page like the following, listing your personal traits, talents, skills, interests, past mentoring experiences, and times when you would be available to perform the role of mentor.

2. Ask a classmate who knows you well and with whom you feel comfortable sharing the information to review your list and add anything you missed.

3. Make copies of your information to take to future mentoring opportunities.

Name: ⁓⁓⁓⁓⁓⁓⁓⁓⁓⁓⁓⁓

Address: ⁓⁓⁓⁓⁓⁓⁓⁓⁓⁓⁓⁓
⁓⁓⁓⁓⁓⁓⁓⁓⁓

Phone Number: ⁓⁓⁓⁓⁓

Personal Traits: ⁓⁓⁓⁓⁓⁓⁓⁓⁓
⁓⁓⁓⁓⁓⁓⁓⁓⁓⁓⁓⁓

Talents: ⁓⁓⁓⁓⁓⁓⁓⁓⁓⁓⁓
⁓⁓⁓⁓⁓⁓⁓⁓

Skills: ⁓⁓⁓⁓⁓⁓⁓⁓⁓⁓⁓⁓
⁓⁓⁓⁓⁓⁓⁓⁓⁓⁓⁓⁓

Interests: ⁓⁓⁓⁓⁓⁓⁓⁓
⁓⁓⁓⁓⁓⁓⁓⁓⁓⁓⁓⁓

Mentoring Experiences: ⁓⁓⁓⁓⁓⁓⁓
⁓⁓⁓⁓⁓⁓⁓⁓⁓⁓⁓⁓

Times Available: ⁓⁓⁓⁓⁓⁓⁓⁓⁓

IN THE NEWS

Respite Services in Mentorship Project

Durham Family Respite Services has received a federal grant for young adults, as mentors, to team with special-needs families in four geographical areas of Durham, Ontario.

The participants of the mentorship project will be working with families who have children with developmental disorders. They will work directly with the families to provide support for the children. This could include strengthening social skills, tutoring, positive peer-interaction, community interaction, educational support, and family relief.

The mentorship project promotes an alternative and cost-effective way for communities to support exceptional families in a "dignified" fashion. It fosters a natural exchange of skills between the families and their children's mentors.

While the families mentor the young adults in areas of job skills, they will in turn support their children in specific areas of their development.

Reprinted by permission of the *Whitby Free Press*.

1. **Why would a mentoring opportunity such as this appeal to young people?**

Activity 2

Mentoring a Younger Person

As a class, brainstorm possible opportunities for you to be a mentor at school, in the community, or in your immediate neighbourhood. As a class, research these possibilities and develop guidelines for the types of mentoring you find. Select a mentoring opportunity that appeals to you and in which you have skills and experience. With permission from home, make the necessary arrangements and volunteer to be a mentor.

Finding a Mentor

Before you begin to look for your own mentor, you have to decide what you want to gain from him or her. You have to decide whether you want to get to know someone new or be with a person whom you already know, respect, trust, and can learn from. Do you want to investigate careers? Do you want to learn more about an industry? Do you want to spend time with someone you admire personally and find out more about him or her? Study this chart to help you decide whom your mentor could be.

WHO/WHAT	GOAL	LOCATION
• Teacher	• Improve attendance • Get better marks	• School
• Service clubs • Social service agencies	• Learn skills • Do volunteer work related to future job	• School • Community
• Employee in your area of career interest	• Experience what it is like on the job	• Workplace
• Educator from an area of educational interest	• Become more informed • Become more aware of skills needed to proceed	• College • University

Activity ③

Defining the Qualities of Mentors

Look over the following list that some students created, of desirable qualities for a mentor.

• Cares about others.
• Listens without judging.
• Advises without lecturing.
• Accepts and values differences.
• Is patient.
• Speaks at a level that is easy to understand.
• Is reliable.
• Wants to make a commitment.
• Is an advocate for others.

Add any other qualities you think are important.

JOURNAL

Contacting a Mentor

Imagine that you are contacting a possible mentor. Choose at least four personal qualities from the list in Activity 3 and tell why they are important to you. Then explain why you would like to have a mentor.

PROFILE

Students Give and Get Career Help

by Paul Luke

The last recession did its best to strangle the ancient art of mentoring. However, Melody Lever, 22, insists on keeping the practice alive because it helped make her what she is—and what she's becoming.

Influenced by a mentor she had as a Grade 10 co-op student at the Vancouver aquarium, Lever decided to enrol in Simon Fraser University's co-op studies program.

Now, a fourth-year biochemistry student on a co-op placement at Vancouver's Terry Fox Labs, Lever has become a mentor herself.

Her protégé is Esther Tang, a 15-year-old student from Burnaby South Secondary School. Tang is one of 45 high school students from the Lower Mainland matched with Simon Fraser University co-op student mentors at 35 workplaces. Participants in the program work four days a week and spend one day taking courses at the university.

A researcher in a medical genetics lab, Lever urges Tang to ask questions, although fielding those questions can prolong her own work day. Lever says mentoring is circular. Even as she supervises Tang, she herself is informally mentored by other researchers in the lab.

Paul Luke/*The Province.*

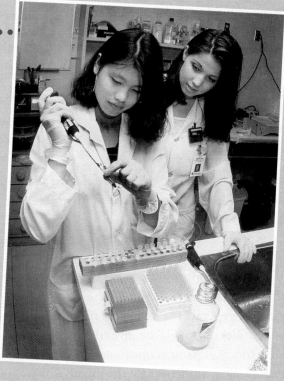

Esther Tang with her mentor, Melody Lever, at Vancouver's Terry Fox Labs.

1. **Why would a recession affect a corporate mentoring program?**

2. **Why does Melody Lever believe in mentoring programs?**

Activity ④

Describing Yourself

Write a description of yourself or create a poster illustrating yourself to give to a mentor. Include what you look like, who is in your family, what your interests are, what your likes, dislikes, goals, and dreams are, and anything else that would help a mentor get to know you better.

Organizations That Provide Mentors

There are many organizations that provide mentors for young people. In the following pages, you can read about these groups and meet some mentors.

Inventor

by The Learning Partnership

Canada has been home to some of the world's greatest inventors: Alexander Graham Bell (telephone), Thomas Ahearn (electric cooking range), Sandford Fleming (standard time), Frederick Banting and Charles Best (insulin). Who are the creative minds of tomorrow who will help Canada remain a world leader in innovation? And what are we doing today to encourage those minds?

The Inventor program matches business mentors with student invention teams from Grades 6, 7, and 8. The volunteer mentors help students identify problems, generate creative ideas for solutions, and develop criteria for evaluating their ideas through the invention of a new product or process.

Partner companies contribute employee time to serve as mentors to the student teams. Students visit the mentor's workplace and apply their inventive skills in a business setting. Back at school, the mentor continues to assist with development of the invention. At the end of the program, students prepare a visual display and oral presentation for an "Invention Convention," at which all teams from participating schools showcase their work. Business mentors review the work, providing recognition and feedback.

Participants develop teamwork, creative-thinking skills, and problem-solving skills in language arts, visual arts, technology, science, business, mathematics, and social studies.

The YMCA's Black Achievers

The YMCA's Black Achievers program links young people with positive role models in the community, according to Annie Bynoe, who co-ordinates the project in Peel Region, Ontario. More than 400 students between the ages of 14 and 21 participate at the six sites operated by the YMCA in the Greater Toronto Area. The program has run in the area for four years. "The program exposes youth to a wide range of educational and career opportunities while raising their academic standards," she said.

Deann Lunan, left, and Leonard Smith, right, with their mentor Juliet Jackson

"The objective is to inspire youth to realize their career goals by linking them with black mentors who are successful in their professions." Bynoe said participants meet twice a month and focus on life skills, career development, and cultural identity.

Deann Lunan, 19, an OAC student at West Hill Collegiate Institute, said she was helped greatly during the three years she's been involved. "I've done a lot of networking with professionals," said Lunan, who is enrolling in a pharmaceutical technology course at Seneca College in Toronto. "It has benefited me a lot. There are a lot of professionals who serve as mentors who I can ask about career decisions."

"It's a really great program," said Juliet Jackson of Brampton, Ontario, a social worker who has volunteered with the project for three years.

Mentors have discussions with between 50 and 60 students during the school year and work to instil feelings of self-respect and the need to achieve.

Leonard Smith, 17, a Grade 12 student at Bramalea Secondary School in Brampton, said he was motivated by the program. "It gives me self-confidence, self-esteem, and makes me work harder to reach my career and goals in life."

Big Sisters

The Big Sisters Associations across Canada assist girls and young women in the development of self-esteem through a voluntary, caring relationship with an adult female volunteer. Little Sisters are referred from a variety of sources: physicians, teachers, public health nurses, social service agencies, parents, and even friends who are Little Sisters themselves. Little Sisters come from a variety of cultural and economic backgrounds. They could live in a single-parent, mother-led family, in a single-parent, father-led family, or in a family in which both parents are present.

"It's lots of fun having a Big Sister," says Little Sister Jenna. "Nancy helps me with my homework sometimes. I want to be a doctor and I know I have to do well in school to become a doctor. I went to Nancy's company Christmas party and got to see where Nancy works. With my Big Sister I get to do things I wouldn't normally do at home."

Volunteers undergo an extensive application and screening process before being matched with a Little Sister. Matches are considered based upon mutual interests and personality traits, among other factors. The Big Sister's major role is being a special friend to a girl who will benefit from the attentions she will receive. Part of the Big Sister's role is to participate in activities with her Little Sister, to share time together, and to develop their friendship. Some Big Sister agencies offer special programs and workshops on issues that are important to girls and young women.

Activity 5

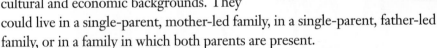

Interviewing Potential Mentors

When you are looking for a suitable mentor, there is some information you will want to find out about the possible candidates when you interview them. Some questions you might wish to ask are:

- Have you ever been a mentor before? Did you enjoy it?
- Would you be interested in being my mentor? If so, why?
- How much time can we spend together and how often?
- Where will we meet?
- Is there anything I can do to contribute to the process?

Create a list of questions, using these and/or questions of your own. Bring them to the interview, along with paper and pen, to make notes about the responses. If you are meeting someone you do not already know, make sure an adult accompanies you.

Activity 6

Role-Playing an Interview

If you have identified potential mentors, you might wish to rehearse your meeting before the interview. Ask a classmate or parent/guardian to role-play the mentor. Set up a situation like the one you expect to encounter. For example, are you meeting at the school guidance office? In a business office? In a restaurant? Gather and arrange any necessary props. Then proceed with your role-play, including greetings, handshakes, introductory conversation, and so on.

Mentors by Mail

What if the person you want as a mentor lives too far away for meetings or even phone calls? An option would be to **correspond**, or exchange letters, with this person. If you both have computers and are on the Internet, you might e-mail each other. In Huron County, Ontario, students are encouraged to communicate with staff and students in other schools as well as mentors in the United States and across Canada. The following mentors offer advice to students who e-mail them with concerns, opinions, or questions.

Dr. Tomorrow, **Frank Ogden**, the distinguished futurist from Vancouver, author of several internationally acclaimed books about technology in our future, such as *Navigating in Cyberspace: A Guide to the Next Millenium*, has agreed to respond to enquiries about how technology is changing our daily lives.

Dr. Constance Edwards, Professional in Alternative Dispute Resolution, of the International Society of Professionals in Alternative Dispute Resolution, has agreed to offer counselling in peer mediation, peace-maker programs, and other matters related to problem solving.

Dick Bolt, a Systems Safety Engineer at NASA's Goddard Space Flight Center, Maryland, U.S.A., has agreed to help kids and teachers find their way around the American NASA space centre (and to entertain questions about his hobbies in antique photography and genealogy).

Activity 7

Writing a Message

Write a message to e-mail to one of the three mentors above. Base your concern, opinion, or question on a situation in your community.

Activity 8

Creating a Home Page

Create a home page for yourself, where you offer advice on a specific topic.

Looking Back

1. Why is mentoring important for some people?

2. What attracts you about participating in a mentoring program?

3. Identify four skills a good mentor should have.

4. Describe two of the mentoring programs in this chapter that appeal to you. Why do you like them?

EXPLORATIONS

Reflections

Look back to Activity 3: Defining the Qualities of Mentors, page 120. Read them over. Write a journal entry about how you can practise these characteristics now.

Goals

What goals do you have for your leisure time when you are an adult? What community activities or organizations do you want to become involved in? Why?

Action!

Imagine that three young people are going to help out as reading buddies in a Grade 3 class. It is their first day.
• A is enthusiastic and excited.
• B is nervous and quiet.
• C is calm and confident.
    In groups of six (three mentors, three Grade 3 students), role-play the walk down the hall, the arrival at the room, and the matching up with reading buddies.

Featuring. . .

Editorial: Write a commentary on the value of after-school programs.

Advertisement: Write an advertisement that outlines the advantages of joining an in-school mentoring program.

Advice Column: Write a letter of advice to a young girl who is planning to quit school as soon as she turns 16. Write it as if you are her teacher, her parent, her younger brother, or her Big Sister.

Research: Look in the Yellow Pages for organizations that provide mentors in your area. Call or write each one for an information package. Publish a summary of the information for your readers.

Personal Story/Interview: Ask your teacher to talk about the three most important people in his or her life at your age.

Experiencing the Community as a Workplace

Now that you have looked more carefully at your community and the people who work in it, you have discovered just what a wide variety and number of tasks there are to be done in a community of any size. After visiting with community members, you realize what an important contribution each one makes. In this part, you will look at how you will fit into the world of work. You have already discovered that you have skills and interests that indicate future careers for you. Now you will have an opportunity to apply them in a real life situation.

Making a Difference in Your Community

What You Will Learn

- To recognize people who have made a difference in their communities.
- To reflect on the importance of teamwork.
- To plan a project that will help people in other communities.
- To create volunteering possibilities for yourself in your community.

Terms to Remember

team   human rights
teamwork   international

Often people get together to do something that makes a difference to the life of their community. The people might be associated with a religion or they might be a group of interested citizens. Sometimes, the task involves raising money to build an arena or a recreational facility. Other times, it involves doing something physical, such as building a ramp for a person with a disability, taking meals to a family that is busy with a crisis, or having a neighbourhood "pitch in" day, when everyone turns out to trim and clean up the community's public places. People enjoy working together on activities like these because it gives them a sense of satisfaction and belonging.

CASE STUDY

Building Spirit from the Ground Up

by Sandra Farran

The residents of Bellvue Manor pitch in to build a park.

Moving 20 tonnes of sand using wheelbarrows pushed by children is probably not the most efficient way to build a park. But the residents of Bellvue Manor in Ottawa's west end would not have had it any other way. For five months, hundreds of volunteers from the community, where roughly half the families receive public assistance, have held bake sales, dart tournaments, garage sales, and car washes. Their goal: to finance a new playground for their children. But the people of Bellvue wanted more than just a place for their kids to have fun. They also hoped to teach them a lesson in the importance of community service—by involving them every step of the way. "I baked banana muffins by myself for a bake sale," says 12-year-old Meagan Robillard. In all, the community raised $34 000. Youth Service Canada, a division of the Federal Human Resources Department, contributed another $23 000 as part of a new nation-wide initiative called Neighbour Aid, whose goal is to encourage community volunteering among Canadian children.

With the fund raising completed, in mid-June 800 men, women, and children rolled up their sleeves for five days of digging, hammering, drilling, and painting. "I baby-sat, worked in the food court, and helped during construction—like handing stuff to adults," says Amanda Moreau, 12. Most of the heavy machinery, including backhoes and trucks, and the professional services of designers and surveyors, were donated or "gotten at a very good deal," says Connor Savage, a consultant for Youth Service Canada. The result: a new park complete with swings, slides, and other playground toys—and a community that has built itself a sense of pride and accomplishment.

Maclean's, July 1, 1996. Reprinted with permission.

1. **What benefits did the children and adults of Bellvue Manor gain from their involvement in this project?**

2. **List projects in your community which could benefit the people who live there.**

A c t i v i t y ① • • • • • • • • • • • • • • • • • **Solving a Community Problem**

Solving a Problem

In the Case Study on page 129, the community had a problem that it wanted to solve. Identify the problem, what people in the community did to raise money, how they worked together during the construction, and what the rewards were when the project was completed. Record your observations in a flowchart like the one at right.

Problem

⬇

Fund-Raising Activities

⬇

Teamwork

⬇

Rewards in the Present

⬇

Goal

⬇

Rewards in the Future

• •

What Is Teamwork?

Community members come together to work as a **team**. In her book, *Games Teams Play*, Leslie Bendaly writes, "A team is a highly effective, cohesive group of individuals who work together with commitment to reach a common goal." It is not enough just to have people working on the same project. They must work together toward a common goal. The following are guidelines for **teamwork** and the roles within a team.

Guidelines for Brainstorming

Defer Decisions!
Do not use put-downs.
Do not make positive or negative judgements.

Opt for Offbeat!
As a thinker, be original.
Try different ways, seek a new combination.

Vast numbers Are Needed!
Go for quantity.
From quantity comes quality.

Expand!
Piggyback or hitchhike on the ideas of others.

Roles Within the Team

The Timekeeper
Do we agree on what to do?
Are we doing what was asked?
Is everyone helping?

The Checker
Have I written down everyone's ideas?
Does everyone understand?
Can everyone explain the answers?

The Cheerleader
Am I keeping the group on track?
Am I smiling and giving the others a thumbs up?
Am I saying, "Good idea!" "Let's go for it!" "Great job!"?

Developed by the Scarborough Board of Education.

When working together as a team, it is very important to be supportive of the other team members, to keep the team focussed on the goal, and to be together in your thinking. The following are some suggestions for behaviour that results in good teamwork.

WANT TO BE A GOOD TEAM PLAYER?

Invite others to talk.

Ask for others' opinions.
Make a plan and stick to it.

Participate by sharing your ideas and information.
Accept responsibility for your task.
Respond to new ideas.
Take time to enjoy the experience.

Open up to other people's feelings.
Follow the ideas of others.

Apply yourself.

Talk about new ideas.
Encourage others.
Appreciate your team members.
Make sure to listen without interrupting.

Activity ②

Creating a Puzzle

Divide into groups. Each group will receive an envelope containing blank puzzle pieces. On each piece, write a rule that will help your group work together as a team. When you are finished, assemble the puzzle.

Team Fitness

It is important that your team "keep fit." As you are working together, ask these questions. (Post them somewhere so that you can all see them.)
• When we work together are we listening to each other?
• Is everyone having a chance to speak?
• Are we feeling proud of our membership on this team?
• Are we focussed?
• Are we sharing the work?
• Are we getting the job done?

CALVIN AND HOBBES © Watterson. Dist. by UNIVERSAL PRESS SYNDICATE.
Reprinted with permission. All rights reserved.

PORTFOLIO

Listing Your Teamwork Skills

Read over the Team Fitness questions. For each one, list the skills that are necessary for answering "yes." For example, if everyone on a team has a chance to speak, it means that team members are co-operating, taking turns, listening, observing, sharing. After you have listed the skills, think about which ones you value most.

Activity 3

Observing Your Community

Over a period of about a week, look around your community for examples of people working together to make things better. Also look for areas or opportunities for you to make a difference. Keep a notebook or tape recorder on hand to record your observations and ideas. Leave room to add to it as you observe more examples. At the end of the time period, combine your ideas as a class and make a master list. Post it on the bulletin board for future use.

Canadian Red Cross

MEALS ON WHEELS

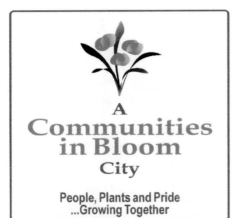

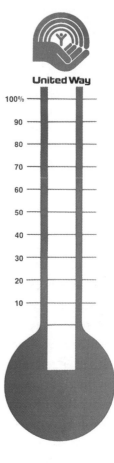

Activity 4

Contacting Community Groups

Choose one of the community projects your class observed in Activity 3 that interests you. Contact the appropriate group or organization by phone, letter, e-mail, or fax, to find out more information about it and the project. When you have received the details, work with your classmates to create a resource list of contacts for future projects.

You might wish to file a copy of the resource list in your portfolio.

Reflecting on Making a Difference

Reflect on small ways in which you can make a difference in your home and school each day. Write five ideas in your journal as steps toward making a difference.

Activity 5

Organizing a Project

When you were observing your community, what needs did you find? Who would you like to help you with a project? How many people could you involve in your "Making a Difference" team? Consider these questions, then follow the outline at right for organizing a project.

Organizing a Project

Identify the problem.

Decide upon a goal.

Find a team of interested workers.

Brainstorm ways to finance the project.

Assign tasks.

Get volunteers involved.

Do it!

IN THE NEWS

The Time of Their Lives

by Dave Finlayson

The pay is $3 a day, you have to be home by 10 p.m. on weekdays, and there's precious little privacy when you're there. Throw in volunteer work evenings and weekends and it's a brutal schedule totally alien to most people. But the young people from across Canada here on the Katimavik program of community service say it's the best experience of their lives.

"It's changed my life. It's put me on the right track," says Dan Nadasdy, 18, of Kitchener, [Ontario]. He's one of nine participants from Ontario, Yukon, Saskatchewan, Quebec, and New Brunswick here on a federal program that lets them work in three different provinces for ten weeks at a time. Nadasdy was in a rut, thinking he would probably end up in the family business of running a group home for schizophrenics, when his mother encouraged him to join the program. Now he's going to be a park ranger. He hasn't worked as a ranger on the program—he's at the Centre for International Alternatives here—but another member of the team has and Nadasdy liked what he saw and heard. He says he wouldn't have even thought about that career if he hadn't joined the program.

Not all the Katimavik participants have such revelations, but all agree the hard work, being

forced to operate together as a cohesive group, and getting to see the country all adds up to a fulfilling experience.

"It's been a blast," says Matt Swain, 20, of Chatham, [Ontario], who took a break before university to join the program, which for this group started in Dalbeau, Quebec, and will end in Wawa, [Ontario]. Swain worked with people with mental disabilities in Quebec— "I don't speak French but it was a great experience"—and is at the River Valley Outdoor Centre here. "Great fun. The people are really friendly."

Edmonton project leader Madeleine Smith isn't surprised at how much young people are getting out of the program. She was a Katimavik participant in 1983 and jumped at the chance to be involved again when the program was resurrected last year. "It had a profound effect on my life. It gave me direction and over the years it's always come back to me."

Katimavik means "meeting place" in [Inuktitut] and the program's goal is to allow young people to experience their country, serve the community, and learn how to work together as a group. It is open to 17- to 21-year-olds who are Canadian citizens or landed immigrants and the participants are a cross-section of society from college graduates to the unemployed.

The program is no paid vacation. It's supposed to teach the

Program co-ordinator Madeleine Smith, in the foreground, is a veteran of the Katimavik program of community service. Behind her are participants holding objects that represent household chores they do.

participants about discipline, cooperation, and community spirit. In any case, the pay doesn't go far. "If you can live on $21 a week, you can change the world," laughs Danika Gallan, 19, of Whitehorse, [Yukon Territory]. "It's not an escape. If you're here to be a slacker, you're not going to like it very much. Sometimes you're so tired of work, you just want to relax but you can't. You learn to keep going even when you don't want to."

The team gets an hour or two break when they get home from their day jobs before they're off on a team project or doing volunteer work. Weekends they've been helping out on such events as dog sled races.

The program is designed to challenge participants. The team has a weekly food budget of $300 they all have to agree on and they also have to make group decisions on a variety of subjects dictated by the program. There's nowhere to hide for young people who've never in their lives had to spend so much time so close to so many other people. "If there's a problem, you have to talk about it and work it out, and that doesn't happen in a lot of families. Some adults could learn from that," Gallan says.

Reprinted by permission of the *Edmonton Journal*.

1. What are the three life skills that young people are supposed to learn during their Katimavik experience?

2. Would you like to join Katimavik? Give reasons for your answer.

3. List the steps that participants should follow so that everyone has a say in how the $300 weekly food budget is spent.

Activity 6

Creating Advertisements

Create a flyer, a poster, a banner, or a button to urge volunteers to help you with your "Making a Difference" project. In the larger presentations, give volunteers a choice of ways to help. Here is a sample flyer from a community group that was starting a breakfast club.

Announcing
The Gold River School Breakfast Express

On Monday, September 15, the Gold River School Breakfast Express will open its doors. This program is available for all students at 8:00 a.m. each day. The Parent Council will co-ordinate the project. They expect to serve 150 students each day at a cost of 50¢ per student. Your support of this breakfast program will be appreciated. Please complete this form and send it to the school office or call the school office to volunteer.

Name_____ Phone _____

Address _____

I want to help because:
❑ my child/children will attend the program.
❑ I believe that breakfast is important for learning.
❑ Other. (Please specify.) _____

_____

I want to help by:
❑ Preparing/serving breakfast one morning a week.
❑ Shopping for the food.
❑ Donating food.
❑ Offering financial support. (A tax-deductible receipt is available.)
❑ Bookkeeping.
❑ Joining the planning committee.
❑ Other. (Please specify.) _____

_____

Thank you for helping us work toward strengthening the bodies and minds of the students at Gold River School, where our children are our future.

The Breakfast Club Committee

PROFILE

Engineering Freedom

by Chris Wood

Vancouver city councillor Sam Sullivan, who gets to the office in a wheelchair, remembers how it was before Paul Cermak's coat hanger. In 1987, a quadriplegic as a result of a skiing accident eight years earlier, Sullivan was living on welfare and desperate to become more independent and employable. But with limited use of his arms and no use of his fingers, he recalls, "I couldn't open the curtains. I couldn't get out the door because of the knob. How could I get a job when I couldn't get out of the door?" He remembers sitting in his room "seething with frustration." Finally, Sullivan wrote to the provincial Association of Professional Engineers, asking if its members could help him. Reply came in the person of Cermak, formerly an engineer with B.C. Hydro and now an independent consultant. The first problem he tackled was in the kitchen, where Sullivan could not hold open his freezer door and remove food at the same time. Cermak solved that with a custom-designed door catch, fashioned from a coat hanger. "Within minutes," Sullivan says, "he revolutionized my life."

Soon, Cermak and other volunteer engineers were finding similarly inventive ways to help other Vancouver-area quadriplegics overcome barriers to independence. Since then, the network of volunteer engineers and technicians making one-of-a-kind "assistive devices," as Sullivan calls them, for people with disabilities, has blossomed beyond all expectations. Formalized in 1992 as the Tetra Society, with Sullivan as its executive director, it now has 37 chapters throughout North America. Last year, the society undertook 1200 projects.

Few were high-tech or expensive. An amber light with a button switch, built in Vancouver for about $20, allows a deaf four-year-old with cerebral palsy to get her teacher's attention without

Sam Sullivan, left, initiated the idea of a Tetra Society. Harry Hardy, right, is a volunteer for it.

having to raise her arm. In London, Ontario, volunteer biomedical engineering students assembled a specialized book rest for a woman with spinal injuries, using scrap wood and 79 cents worth of hardware. Says Harry Hardy, a retired machine designer who recently completed his twentieth project for the society, "I enjoy figuring out the problem and what they need to solve it. It's always nice to see how happy a person is after it's done, how they can do something for themselves that they couldn't do before." It is a joy of accomplishment that Sullivan, who won his municipal office in 1993, shares and understands.

Maclean's, July 1, 1996. Reprinted with permission.

1. Who belongs to the Tetra Society? What is the Tetra Society's purpose?

2. How did a coat hanger begin "engineering freedom" for Sam Sullivan?

3. Make drawings or plans for a device to help a person who cannot bend over to tie his or her shoes.

Activity  7

Creating a Collage

With a partner, collect magazines and newspapers that contain articles or photographs about people who have made a difference in their communities. Create a collage of words and images that reflect their actions.

Activity 8

Making a Difference

Research one person of interest to you who really made a difference in his or her community. Write a descriptive poem, profile, or song, draw a picture, or take a photograph. Show what he or she did to make a difference. Put it on one page. When everyone has finished the assignment, tape the pages together to create a class book entitled "People Who Made a Difference."

Making a Difference Beyond Your Community

Improved travel and communications have made the world seem smaller. Today we are more aware of the problems in communities outside of our own. We see that one cannot be isolated, and that the problems of poverty, disease, homelessness and the denial of **human rights** are everywhere. Some organizations are looking for ways to give young people an opportunity to help with **international** issues, meaning issues among nations. Here are some ideas to get you thinking.

• Contact the Canadian Foundation for World Development. Collect used eyeglasses from your friends, relatives, and neighbours and send them to this organization. They distribute them, and other items, to people in developing countries.

- Contact Oxfam for a fund-raising and information kit. Your class can learn about the needs of developing countries and raise money to help.
- Contact UNICEF for a fund-raising kit. It includes stickers, posters, buttons, and ideas for planning fund-raising events throughout the year. The money goes to programs in 120 developing countries.
- Invite a group from the International Youth for Peace and Justice Tour to make a presentation to your school.
- Contact Amnesty International to find out how to participate in one of their letter-writing campaigns for the release of "prisoners of conscience," people who are imprisoned without just cause.
- Collect children's books in good condition and send them to schools in developing countries.

    These are just a few of many organizations which work internationally to improve people's lives. There are many more organizations, and many ways in which you could help. You could:

- Visit your library to get lists of similar organizations.
- Ask people in those organizations to give you information on others.
- Check your guidance office for information on international youth volunteer programs.
- Ask your local religious groups for information on programs they might be involved in.
- Watch for reports of aid to developing countries in newspapers and magazines.
- Contact the office of your member of parliament for information.

Activity  9

Planning a Project

Work with three or four of your classmates to develop a strategy for carrying out one of these projects.

 You might wish to file a copy of the strategy in your portfolio.

Looking Back

1. What steps are needed to organize a project?

2. List five guidelines for good teamwork.

3. Give three examples of ways people help in your community.

4. Give three examples of ways you can help people in the global community.

5. Which activity did you enjoy the most in this chapter? Why?

EXPLORATIONS

Reflections

Describe in your journal where you would like to be in ten years. What would you like to be doing? What steps will you take to get there? Who else will be involved?

Goals

List some of the ways in which you would like to make a difference for yourself and others in the future. Include goals that have local and worldwide impact.

Action!

Choose one of the programs described in this chapter. Imagine that you are making a speech about the program to a group of people who are going to donate funds to the project. List the points that you want to make. Make the "pitch" to a group of your classmates.

Featuring. . .

Editorial: Write an editorial on the importance of people in communities working together to bring about change.

Advice Column: Write a letter of advice about teamwork to Grade 4 students who are getting ready to plan a Winter Carnival Day for the Kindergarten class.

Advertisement: Create an advertisement promoting one of the projects or organizations outlined in this chapter.

Personal Story/Interview: Interview, and tell the personal story, of someone in your family, school, or community who worked on a local project in the past.

Research: Contact the local Canadian Red Cross Society, or read about the organization, and find out how they help relatives who have lost touch to get together. Write an article about your findings.

Connecting in Your Community

What You Will Learn

- What job shadowing is and the procedures involved in it.
- What volunteer activities are available in your community and what skills you have as a potential volunteer.
- How to increase your involvement in the school community.
- How to create your own volunteer experience.

Terms to Remember

job shadowing
volunteer training programs
volunteer co-ordinators

There are many ways to make connections in your community. In the last chapter, you found out more about what makes your community function. You might have discovered information that was new to you, especially in the area of the actual jobs that people do. Now you can choose to make a stronger connection and learn even more by spending time volunteering, job shadowing, and working in your community.

Job Shadowing

Does participating in a **job shadowing** experience for a day interest you? Job shadowing means spending a day at work with a person in a particular career, at a particular job that interests you. During the day, you will observe what the job involves, talk to other employees, and, with permission, take pictures at the site. Your school might already do this as a part of Career Week or to encourage students to participate in a co-operative education program. Job shadowing—in places like hospitals, trucking depots, design studios, auto repair shops, banks, news rooms, or offices—is exciting, and an excellent learning opportunity.

This type of experience has recently become popular across Canada through the Take Our Kids to Work day which is held in November.

Activity 1

Preparing Questions

When you are job shadowing, you could ask some of the same questions you asked your community visitors. (See Chapter 7, page 97.) Or, you could design a Know-Want-Learn (KWL) Chart as your guide.

The Know-Want-Learn Chart   Topic _____

What do I already **Know** about __'s job?	What do I **Want** to know about __'s job?	What did I **Learn** about __'s job?
_____	_____	_____
_____	_____	_____
_____	_____	_____
_____	_____	_____
_____	_____	_____
_____	_____	_____
_____	_____	_____
_____	_____	_____

You could also make up your own questions. Keep in mind that people respond in different ways to different types of questions. There are four types for your purposes. Look at these samples to see which type gives the most information.

1. Yes/No questions
These can be answered simply and give little information. For example, "Do you like your work?"

2. Fact-finding questions
These are specific and give more information. For example, "What four things make your work challenging? What do you like most? What do you like least?"

3. Open-ended questions
These questions are more personal and can lead to more questions. For example, "What are the things you like about your job? How did you get started in this job? What do you need to know to be successful in your job?"

4. Follow-up questions
These questions are used to get more information or to clarify an answer. They keep the conversation going. For example, "That's interesting. Can you tell me more?"

TIPS FOR A GREAT INTERVIEW

✔ Prepare the questions you want to ask the person at work.

✔ Ask the most important question first, in case you run out of time.

✔ Listen carefully. Give the person your full attention.

✔ Ask "Why is that?" or "Please tell me more" when you want to know more.

✔ Tell about your own experience that relates to something he or she tells you.

✔ Jot down specific information.

✔ Write up your notes afterwards.

✔ Thank the person for his or her time.

IN THE NEWS

School Kids Rise'n'shine to Shadow Work World

By Dennis Hryciuk

Wide hallways lead 13-year-old Daniel St. Gelais past what might seem like familiar institutional settings—a cafeteria, a small library, laboratories. But Daniel knows he isn't going to hear the bells ringing for lunch or class breaks. This is no school. This is the work world of his future step-father Bob Tower and everything else about it is as unfamiliar to Daniel as the electron microscopes he's about to view.

It's a world that educators hope Daniel and other students become more familiar with after taking part in a new Canada-wide program. Called Take Our Kids to Work, the program encourages students to spend an entire day at a parent's workplace or at a sponsoring organization. Daniel and about 200 other Grade 9 students at S. Bruce Smith junior high school did just that, with an estimated 250 000 others in communities across the country.

For Daniel, that meant accompanying Tower on his rounds as a researcher at the Alberta Research Council—starting with an earlier than usual awakening at 6:30 a.m. Tower took Daniel to a corporate client that manufactures paint-removing pellets from ground-up waste materials. Using a blast nozzle, Daniel got to try removing paint from a large test piece of aluminum. "It was neat," Daniel said, in what was to be rather sparse conversation from a tired-looking student. The highlights were mixed with boring stuff, he admitted. "Writing things like proposals. I could live with that if I got to do the fun stuff, too."

Good at science and math, Daniel said he'd like a career in science but hasn't decided much beyond that. "It takes your brain, especially in this kind of work. Technology is changing so fast it's hard to keep up."

They sounded like familiar words and Tower nodded his head in approval. The researcher-parent said he arranged his day to include both Daniel and a company visit to show how varied his own job is. Tower helps companies develop and test products for clients, and has been working at the research council for 20 years. It's a job he clearly loves, explaining the finest details of scientific computer graphs.

Daniel's story is one of many that students are involved in as part of their career education, said S. Bruce Smith school-teacher Mike Wilkie. Some students were shocked that they had to get up so early in the morning to accompany their parents,

Bob Tower, right, shows his stepson Daniel St. Gelais around the Alberta Research Council.

Wilkie said. "I think there will be quite an awakening for some. And this won't be some fun day off," the teacher said.

Students spent class time preparing for their visits and will complete assignments dealing with their experiences. And while some students might be as lucky as Daniel to visit someone with an unusual and well-paying job, others might experience quite the opposite. "I think some kids could go out with parents with minimal paying jobs," said Mary-Lou Cleveland, principal at Steele Heights Junior High. "Then they might say, 'Hey, I'd better study!'"

Reprinted by permission of the *Edmonton Journal*.

1. **Discuss Daniel's observations about his stepfather's job.**

Recording Your Job-Shadowing Day

A day planner could be used to record an hour-by-hour, task-by-task description of your job-shadowing day. It would also be an excellent keepsake of your experience and a handy reference when answering your classmates' questions about your day.

There are other ways to share your day: a talk show, a photo essay, a newspaper article, a report, or a video or audio tape.

File the material on your job-shadowing day in your portfolio.

Activity 2

Evaluating the Day

Here is a guide to use after your job-shadowing day to share your experiences, in groups, with your classmates.

1. Whom did you "shadow"?

2. What is his or her job?

3. What other jobs did you find out about?

4. What did you like about the day?

5. What did you dislike?

6. In your opinion, how could the day have been improved?

7. What did you learn?

8. What else would you like to say?

Volunteering in the Community

Like job shadowing, volunteering offers you another unique experience. It is not about learning from books. It is learning by being around different people, doing things that you would not normally do, and seeing things from a different point of view. By volunteering, you will have a chance to exercise your independence, assume more responsibility, negotiate with adults on a more equal footing, and gain employability skills. You will have the opportunity to develop your own identity, based on what you can do and what special gifts you have. Volunteering also helps solve the problem of "I need a job to get experience. I need experience to get a job."

FOR BETTER OR FOR WORSE © Lynn Johnston Prod., Inc. Reprinted with permission of UNIVERSAL PRESS SYNDICATE. All rights reserved.

When you consider volunteering, four questions need to be asked:
- What skills can I offer?
- What skills do I want to gain?
- What group do I want to work with?
- What time do I have available?

Being a volunteer usually involves committing to a specific time each week for helping out at an organization or community service. Some examples are:
- Going to a seniors' residence to visit or play games with seniors.
- Sorting food at a local food bank.
- Helping at a day-care centre.
- Cleaning up an area of the environment.
- Providing special-occasion events for children in hospitals.

Create a list of volunteer activities in which you would like to participate.

Many organizations have **volunteer training programs** and **volunteer co-ordinators**. Most have a contact person for you to call to set up an appointment. You can find out how to get in touch with these people in your local Yellow Pages or, in some cases, on the Internet.

Some national organizations you might wish to contact for a list of their local branches are:

Volunteer Canada

Canadian Centre for Philanthropy (charity)

United Way of Canada-*Centraide Canada*

YMCA Canada

Canadian Environmental Network

Canadian Parks and Recreation Association

Canadian Association for Community Care

Community Foundations of Canada

Canadian Conference for the Arts

Activity  3 ●

Creating a Bulletin Board Display

In a group or individually, create a bulletin board display, under the heading "How Can You Help?" Create a picture for each example of ways to help in the community. Explain each image on the board in an oral presentation to the class. You might wish to invite other classes to the presentation to encourage them to get involved in the activities.

CASE STUDY

Connect the Dots

by Janice Turner

They began as cast members. Today, they're advocates [champions]. They're three Metro-area kids who starred in a film celebrating cultural diversity. Now they want no less than to make the world a better place.

Peter Chow, Patrick Herman, and Mandy Pipher work on a mural for the Little Red Dot Club.

"We wanted to help this movie along," says Mandy Pipher, 12, co-chair of the newly formed Little Red Dot Club. "We didn't want to let the message of the movie die. It just isn't any old movie. It's a good tool."

The film, *Just a Little Red Dot*, premiered at the Ontario Science Centre in June, 1996. It's based on an incident that took place at a public school in May 1994.

One day, a Grade 5 student gave her teacher a package of red dots *(bindis)* as a birthday present. Several youngsters in the class thought the stick-on dots were rather neat, and decided to put them on. But when they went outside for recess, they were met with laughter and ridicule.

The Grade 5 youngsters became determined to teach the whole school about the *bindi*, a decorative dot worn by some East Indian and Sri Lankan women. In their mission to change student attitudes, the kids affectionately dubbed the adornment the "cool dot."

Once worn to indicate that a woman was married, today the dot is more commonly worn as a fashion or make-up accessory.

"It took a great deal of courage and boldness for these children to try to overcome their peers' racist attitudes," recalls Mitra Sen, the teacher who received the *bindis* as a gift. "But in time their message began to spread. . . . I remember the sight when almost half the children in the school were wearing these little red dots. This little sym-bol, which was once viewed so negatively, had taken on a whole new meaning. . . . It was now respected and appreciated." Sen, who was assistant director of the hit TV series *Degrassi Junior High* before becoming a teacher, helped turn the incident into a half-hour docudrama.

Mandy, co-chair Patrick Herman, 13, and art director Peter Chow, 12, were among the film's 80 young cast members. They spent much of the summer on the phones, computers, and faxes planning club activities for the school year. They plan to take their message of diversity and understanding to junior schools throughout Ontario and, eventually, across Canada. "Our goal is to make our generation realize the importance of sharing and understanding different cultures so that when we grow up, we will know how to co-operate with all people no matter what they look like or where they come from," say club members in their brochure.

Reprinted with permission—The Toronto Star Syndicate.

1. What character traits does this group exemplify?

2. What do you admire most about these young people?

3. What do they make you realize about your peers?

Strengthening the School Community

One place to start getting involved as a volunteer in your community is within your school. You have probably been part of a fund-raising committee or a school team. You might also have also been a bus captain, a reading buddy, a peer mediator, or a lunchroom helper. By participating, you widen your own learning and improve the community in which you spend so much time.

Activity  4

Creating Volunteer Positions

Work with your teachers and classmates to widen the scope of volunteer positions within your school. Here are some possibilities:

- Setting up the gym for Phys. Ed.
- Setting up for assembly programs.
- Delivering information to classrooms.
- Answering the telephone while staff has a break or lunch.
- Going on excursions with younger students.
- Assisting with play-day activities.
- Hosting school visitors.
- Becoming peer assistants for yard duty.
- Unpackaging and distributing supplies.
- Greeting and taking new students on a school tour.
- Becoming primary-grade helpers.
- Becoming a peer mediator or tutor.
- Serving on the Student Council.
- Becoming a game official, scorekeeper, or timer for school sports.
- Acting as a crossing guard before and after school each day.

Activity 5

Recognizing In-School Volunteer Activities

In-school volunteer activities could be recognized in a number of ways. You might wish to form a committee of students, teachers, and parents who want to enhance the in-school volunteer opportunities. Work together to do some, or all, of the following:

- Create a directory of volunteer opportunities at your school.
- Develop records or a database on which volunteers' activities and hours are kept.
- Develop a certificate to award students who contribute over 50 hours per year.
- Hold sharing sessions for volunteers to discuss what works and what does not.
- At the end of the year, hold a training session for younger students who will be moving into your grade or school.

PROFILE

Stephanie Trim—Playground Mediator

by Merle MacIsaac

If a playground dispute lands in the principal's office at William King Elementary School just outside Halifax, Nova Scotia, chances are that the students brought it there. And just as likely, the kids will iron out the problem themselves through a mediation process— without adult intervention. "It really works," says Stephanie Trim, an 11-year-old Grade 5 student acting as an on-duty mediator. Trim's classmates nominated her to attend two days of mediation training last fall in nearby Truro. They judged her to be a good listener, an essential quality in a process in which opponents agree to tell their version of a problem honestly, describe their feelings, and work out a solution. "The hardest part," Trim says of her role, "was learning not to give advice. They have to figure it out for themselves."

As in many schools across Canada, mediation is part of a broader program of instruction in peaceful living at William King. Principal Hetty Adams believes that punishment fails to address the cause of many playground problems. Unresolved, those disputes can escalate and undermine the learning environment.

Trim has witnessed the results of Adams's approach. Recently, a fight between two boys turned out to be a dispute over privacy: one had read excerpts from the other's diary without permission. Trim convinced the guilty party to apologize, and to stop telling others about what he had read. Like adult mediation, the program at William King requires that "disputants" agree to try to solve the problem, and to tell the truth, without interruptions or put-downs. The mediators must respect the confidentiality of the parties,

Stephanie Trim, playground mediator at William King Elementary School in Halifax, with Principal Hetty Adams.

listen carefully, and remain impartial. "You can't just slouch in the chair," says Trim. "That would mean you don't care what they're saying. And you really can't say, 'Omigosh, he did that?'"

Maclean's, May 20, 1996. Reprinted with permission.

1. Discuss the qualities of a good mediator.

2. Identify the guidelines in the article used to mediate a dispute, then brainstorm others that you think would be important.

3. Have you played the role of mediator before? Describe your experience, your reactions, and your feelings. Did you enjoy the experience? You might wish to file this account in your portfolio.

Creating Your Own Volunteer Experience

Perhaps you do not want to make a long-term, weekly volunteer commitment but you still want to gain experience as a volunteer. Here is an idea that could work for you. Watch the local newspapers for announcements of upcoming events. When you see one that interests you, telephone the organizers of the event and volunteer your services. Make a list of what you can and are willing to do, and let them know. Be sure to discuss your plans with your parents or guardians. Depending on your talents, skills, and available time, the volunteer activities might include those listed at right.

If you do not feel comfortable calling someone you do not know, create a similar list of how you can help and pass it out to family friends. Perhaps they will be involved in an event at which your services could be used.

> **Possible Volunteer Activities**
>
> *Before the Event*
> • Delivering handbills
> • Making posters
> • Phoning
>
> *On the Day of the Event*
> • Unloading supplies
> • Setting up tables or displays
> • Giving information
> • Being a guide
>
> *After the Event*
> • Packing up
> • Dismantling tables or displays
> • Cleaning up

PORTFOLIO

Creating a Thank-You Card

Create a thank-you card for the organizers of the event you helped with. Let them know what you learned by helping. If you really enjoyed it and want to repeat the experience, ask to be a part of the planning for the next event. Ask if a thank-you letter from them could be given to you for your portfolio.

Keep these letters in your portfolio, along with a list of tasks you performed and your reflections on the day. They might help you in the future.

JOURNAL

Reflecting on Your Experience

At the end of a day of volunteering, write about your experience in your journal. Use the following guideline so that you consider all aspects of the day.

Today I worked as a volunteer at . . .
The best part was . . .
One thing I learned was . . .
I think others appreciated the fact that I . . .
The next time I volunteer to help with an event, I will be sure to . . .

Another way of reflecting on your experience is to complete a Response Wheel. Beginning at 1, ask yourself these questions:

1. What did I see and hear?
2. How did I feel?
3. What did it make me think about?
4. What action could I take or what could I do as a result of this?

My Response to Volunteering

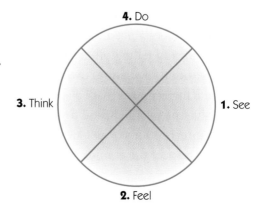

Looking Back

1. List four ways that you can broaden your experience in the world of work.

2. Name three volunteer experiences that interest you. Explain why.

3. Describe what you and your classmates can do to become involved in your school community.

EXPLORATIONS

Reflections

Comment on the following statement: "You never get a second chance to make a first impression." Why is this valuable to remember?

Goals

How have your experiences in the community strengthened, or changed, your goals for the future?

Action!

In groups of three, create skits with the following themes:

- Introducing your best friend to an adult whom you have met through volunteering.
- Telling your parent or guardian about your job-shadowing experience.
- Convincing your friend that he or she should join you at your after-school volunteering placement.
- Apologizing for forgetting to inform someone who was consequently inconvenienced that you would be absent.

Featuring. . .

Editorial: Write an editorial that outlines the importance of young people finding out more about the people who work in their community. Assume that some of your readers think that the best place for children to learn is in the classroom.

Advice Column: Write a letter advising a new student who has recently moved into the area about the local opportunities for learning in the community.

Advertisement: Create an advertisement for student volunteer opportunities in your school. Ask school staff members for a description of the help they require and how to get involved.

Personal Story/Interview: Meet with the Advertising Team and interview the staff members who want volunteers about the type of program they run and why a volunteer would enjoy the experience. Try to represent a variety of programs.

Research: Call local agencies and create a Volunteers Wanted column in your magazine that lists opportunities for student volunteers outside of school hours.

Putting Your Skills to Work

What You Will Learn

- To evaluate what you learned while working in the community.
- To identify your transferable skills.
- To relate your transferable skills to job choices.
- How to write a résumé or fact sheet.
- How to create a personal profile.

Terms to Remember

transferable skills
consult
problem solving
résumé

fact sheet
character references
personal profile

I n this chapter, you will learn to identify your employability skills, update your skills inventory, and relate your skills to possible career choices. This will prepare you for writing a résumé, a fact sheet, or a personal profile. All of these things will build your confidence in approaching the work force.

FOR BETTER OR FOR WORSE © Lynn Johnston Prod., Inc. Reprinted with permission of UNIVERSAL PRESS SYNDICATE. All rights reserved.

Top Ten Skills and Attitudes

Make a chart similar to the sample that follows. On the left side, write employers' top ten skills and attitudes. On the right side, write the experience(s) you have had in the community to strengthen that skill.

Employers' Top Ten	MY TOP TEN
1. Positive attitude	- Packed boxes at the food bank.
2. Dependable	- Said I'd help my friend with his science project and I did.
3. Self-motivated	- Was interested in volunteering at the Red Cross and called them to offer my services.
4. Shows initiative	- Suggested a better way of organizing a class project.
5. Good self-esteem	- Wasn't nervous talking to new people at the Red Cross blood donor clinic.
6. Basic skills - numeracy	- Kept track of funds raised for a community project.
- literacy	- Read materials on various volunteer organizations to know which ones I wanted to become involved in.
- computer literacy	- Used a software program to keep track of the funds for the community project.
7. Works well with others	- Received many compliments on my helpful behaviour from people I worked with at the food bank.
8. Good communication skills	
9. Honest	- Was trusted with the funds raised for the class community project.
10. Good decision-making skills	

PORTFOLIO

Creating a Community Action Report

Reflecting on your learning in an organized way will help you see how many skills can be practised in a variety of experiences. You might prefer to complete a more open-ended chart than compare your skills to the Top Ten. Divide a sheet of paper as shown here. On the left side, write the statements as shown. Write your reflections on the right side.

If you are reporting on an activity that you did with a group (such as Organizing a Project, page 133), alter the statements to reflect the team's experience. Reports such as these will help you by confirming what skills you are using.

COMMUNITY ACTION REPORT	
Experience	*REFLECTIONS*
What I did	- *I contacted people and collected items from them for a garage sale for the Young Variety group.*
How I did it	- *I phoned people and, with my dad's help, picked up the items.*
How I feel	- *I feel like I accomplished something worthwhile on my own.*
Who I worked with	- *Glenn Lucas and other people from Young Variety.*
A highlight for me	- *Getting positive remarks about my efforts.*
What is next	- *Working with Young Variety on their next project.*

IN THE NEWS

Jobs Without Pay

by Janice Turner

You weren't able to get a summer job or the job you did get hasn't exactly been rewarding. If this sounds all too familiar, maybe it's time you thought about volunteering. That's what more than 500 students in the Metro Toronto area alone have been doing for the past two months through the Canadian Red Cross. The organization offers youth opportunities in such areas as fund-raising, research and writing, administration, community service, and

Michael Mohammed chats with fellow Red Cross volunteer Vicky Tan. "I love administrative stuff," says Michael, who is managing more than a dozen other students. "It's fun."

leadership. Janet Gunn, co-ordinator of training and development for the Metro Toronto branch of the society, says volunteering gives students a chance to add to their résumés, as well as develop new skills and meet interesting people.

Between 500 and 700 students aged 14 and up have been placed annually with the organization since the summer program took off four years ago in 1993. Opportunities are publicized in high schools early in the year. Recruiting takes place in May and June. Placements included sales clerks, bike safety leaders, blood donor clinic helpers, data entry clerks, office assistants, food bank volunteers, caretakers, driving companions, and registration clerks. The Red Cross also runs a year-round program for young volunteers.

Michael Mohammed, who just turned 17, has spent 15 to 20 hours a week this summer co-ordinating other young volunteers at various North York blood donor clinics. He has also contributed to the summer program's student newsletter. Last year he was one of the students responsible for customer service—serving juice and cookies at clinics, ensuring that donors were well taken care of. This summer he's managing more than a dozen other students. Both this year and last he has tried to find a summer job, but with no luck. So, rather than be idle, Michael is doing something he considers useful and challenging. Sure, it would be nice to get a paycheque. He's hoping his volunteer experience will lead to paid work down the road.

"I'm doing this for the experience—and it's fun," Michael says, during a break from a recent clinic. "I get to organize things. I love administrative stuff. I'm managing a project and managing people. It takes up a fair bit of my time, but it also leaves me time for a social life."

As well, twice a month he visits day camps to talk to youngsters aged 7 to 12 about Red Cross international development issues. Michael notes that if he didn't have to worry about university tuition, he'd volunteer indefinitely. Still, he points out that volunteering is not for everyone. Your heart, he emphasizes, has to be in it. "You can't just put in the hours to get a few lines on your résumé," he says. "You have to do a good job while you're at it."

What do you need to qualify? Enthusiasm, an eagerness to learn, and a desire to contribute to the greater good, Gunn says.

"We look for people who are flexible, who have a really positive attitude, and who understand what commitment means," she stresses. "We find out what we can provide that will satisfy the student and what the student will provide that will satisfy us."

During the summer, most youngsters commit to about five hours a week; many opt for more. For some of the younger students, volunteering may be the only really structured routine they have. For many older students, volunteering is something they do in addition to going to summer school or holding down a summer job. Whereas the Red Cross sees the program as a way to foster community and team involvement from an early age, students tend to view it as a chance to acquire people skills and earn references.

Reprinted with permission—The Toronto Star Syndicate.

1. In small groups, identify the positions available through the Red Cross summer program on the left side of a sheet of paper. Then, brainstorm all the skills that would be gained by performing that job. Record these on the right side of the page.

2. Tell which job you would prefer to do and why.

Transferable Skills

Transferable skills is a term that is being used more and more these days as technology forces people to change careers, as people who have been at home as caregivers return to an altered workplace, and as "retired" people take jobs in new areas. Transferable skills are the skills you already have that can be applied to a new situation. For example, many students exhibit leadership skills in the sports they play. They realize that before they can be a good leader, they must be a good follower. They realize that all team members must be **consulted**, or have an opportunity to offer their opinion and be listened to. Consulting is a transferable skill that is valuable throughout your lifetime. Another example of a transferable skill is **problem solving**. If you are a person who approaches the problem of an unco-operative computer or a lost math text calmly and with resolve, you will probably handle the broken fax machine and the lost invoice at the workplace in the same way. The chart that follows shows examples of skills learned at home or school that could be applied at work.

Transferable Skills Chart

SKILL	EXAMPLES AT HOME/SCHOOL	EXAMPLES IN THE WORKPLACE
Communication	• math tutor • reading buddy • newsletter editor	• explain concepts to others • read with understanding • write persuasively
Interpersonal	• community club volunteer • peer mediator • new student welcome wagon volunteer	• express feelings appropriately • withstand and resolve conflict • sensitive to cultural differences
Leadership	• basketball team member • peer mediating co-chair • YMCA camp counsellor	• appreciate/reward peers' efforts • bring reason to a problem • motivate others
Problem Solving	• alter recycled clothing • worked out a scheduling conflict at home	• see all sides of a situation • open-minded
Adaptability	• changed schools twice • created new system of team playoffs	• accept change as a challenge • tackle problems with optimism

Self-management	• use a planner • earn own spending money • prepare meals	• demonstrate the need to achieve • resourceful • creative
Initiative	• found own mentor • started baby-sitting co-op	• identify untried possibilities • carry out ideas

Activity  1 ·····································

Identifying Your Transferable Skills

Create a chart similar to the one in the example, and fill in your own experiences from home or school that could be applied to a workplace. You might wish to consult a friend or a parent or guardian to determine your skills. Use the same skills listed, if they apply to you, and add any others from the following Employability Skills list that reflect your abilities.

Employability Skills Profile: The Critical Skills Required of the Canadian Workforce

ACADEMIC SKILLS	PERSONAL MANAGEMENT SKILLS	TEAMWORK SKILLS
Those skills which provide the basic foundation to get, keep, and progress on a job and to achieve the best results.	The combination of skills, attitudes, and behaviours required to get, keep, and progress on a job and to achieve the best results.	Those skills needed to work with others on a job to achieve the best results.
Canadian employers need a person who can: **Communicate** • Understand and speak in the languages in which business is conducted. • Listen to understand and learn. • Read, comprehend, and use written materials, including graphs, charts, and displays. • Write effectively in the languages in which business is conducted.	**Canadian employers need a person who can demonstrate:** **Positive Attitudes and Behaviours** • Self-esteem and confidence. • Honesty, integrity, and personal ethics. • A positive attitude toward learning, growth, and personal health. • Initiative, energy, and persistence to get the job done.	**Canadian employers need a person who can:** **Work with Others** • Understand and contribute to the organization's goals. • Understand and work within the culture of the group. • Plan and make decisions with others and support the outcomes. • Respect the thoughts and opinions of others in the group. • Exercise "give and take" to achieve group results. • Seek a team approach as appropriate. • Lead when appropriate, mobilizing the group for high performance.

Think
- Think critically and act logically to evaluate situations, solve problems, and make decisions.
- Understand and solve problems involving mathematics and use the results.
- Use technology, instruments, tools, and information systems effectively.
- Access and apply specialized knowledge from various fields (e.g., skilled trades, technology, physical sciences, arts, and social sciences).

Responsibility
- The ability to set goals and priorities in work and personal life.
- The ability to plan and manage time, money, and other resources to achieve goals.
- Accountability for actions taken.

Learn
- Continue to learn for life.

Adaptability
- A positive attitude toward change.
- Recognition of and respect for people's diversity and individual differences.
- The ability to identify and suggest new ideas to get the job done—creatively.

Activity 2

Relating Your Skills to Possible Careers

When you identify your transferable skills, you can relate them to some of the careers in the Career Clusters in Chapter 6, page 75. Before you do this, gain some practice by using the example at right. From the Employability Skills Profile, choose the skills you think are required for the sample occupations. You may use each skill more than once. Write your chart on a piece of paper.

Job	SKILLS REQUIRED
Recreation Director	- accept responsibility
	- motivate others
	- have a strong self-image
	- speak effectively
Musician	
Telecommunications Installer	
Banker	
Chef	
Dietitian	
Publisher	
Auto Mechanic	

Activity 3

Imagining Me and You in a Career

With a partner, review the Career Clusters on page 75. Choose one that contains jobs that interest you. Tell your partner which one it is. Your partner will then choose a career or job that he or she can imagine you in and tell you why, keeping your transferable skills and interests in mind.

Example:
If you enter the Business and Marketing field, I can imagine you working in travel and tourism because you have excellent interpersonal skills, pay attention to details, and like learning new things.

Continue this activity for the four career clusters.

Activity 4

Creating an "Imagine Me . . . Imagine You" Display

As a class, divide a bulletin board into four quadrants and label each one with a career cluster heading. Then make a cartoon outline of yourself. On it, write your name, career choice, and the skills you now have that you will be able to use on the job. Post it on the bulletin board under the appropriate career-cluster heading.

JOURNAL

Imagining Your Future

In words or drawings, outline the impact your job choice(s) will have on you 15 years from now. Use the headings:
- Work location
- Home location
- Type of accommodation
- Family situation
- Leisure activities

PROFILE

● ●

Pure Excitement

"We describe it as a cross between a roller coaster and a lottery. You never know how crazy the ride's going to be. You just take your chances, put your quarter in, and go for it." This analogy by Vancouver's Jordy Birch, lead singer of the band Pure, sums up more than six years of experience in both the local and international music scene. It conveys what many people know about the music industry: that it's a tough way to make a living, with a lot of unexpected twists and turns. But it also resounds with a feeling of excitement. There is energy in Canada's music industry, and it's heard in local bands like Pure. "It's a good business," says Birch, "because it's always changing, always getting more interesting."

Interesting it may be, but over the years Birch and his band-mates have recognized that today's music industry is, indeed, a business. And while ability in music is a primary requirement, it takes more than high school music classes to make it in this talent show.

Pure's talent for penning upbeat tunes and for recording and self-producing them is what got the band their first contract with the American label Reprise Records in 1991. It's also what got them out of that deal after releasing two albums and an EP. "We always had this plan to get out and have our own record company. Finally we did because it made more sense," says Birch. "We bought a studio, we were completely debt-free, and we started Shag."

Shag is Pure's record label. And it is through Shag Records that the members of Pure have been able to bring together all of the skills they have learned during their years in business, mixing music with art, science, and production, to create CDs they can completely call their own. "We like to do a lot of things, rather than just one thing. We're playing music pretty much all the time, but we're also doing album covers, taking care of the record company business, and touring," says Birch. Not to mention recording, engineering, and producing their own albums, as well as maintaining their personal web site.

All that work may sound different from the typical musician's lifestyle that's often glamorized on *MuchMusic*, but according to Birch, it's a reality of the business. "Sure there are a lot of fun things to do, but it is a lot of work too," he says.

It is, however, a reality that has become very fulfilling to Birch. "I like it when it all comes together. When we've created something and we can actually go on tour and show off what we've done. That's always the best part."

Reprinted with permission of *Career Paths* 1996, published by YES Canada-BC and funded by Human Resources Development Canada and the BC Ministry of Education, Skills and Training.

1. In small groups, list all the areas of the music industry that Pure is involved with and identify the skills the members have, collectively, to maintain their business.

2. Make a list of other performers with whom you are familiar. What skills do they have that help them to maintain their popularity?

Looking at Yourself on Paper

Whether you are looking for a volunteer placement or a paid position, whether you want to work on a regular or a casual basis, the people you will be working with will want to know some facts about you.

Résumé or Fact Sheet

Personal facts and experiences are usually written into a **résumé** or a **fact sheet**. They provide valuable information about you for the people with whom you will be working.

    Résumés and fact sheets usually require the following information:

Name
Address (including postal code)
Phone number
Current grade level
School's name and address
Relevant experiences
Memberships
Awards/Certificates
Interests
Character references (Names and phone numbers of people who know you well or whom you have worked with who can confirm your experiences.)

Activity 5

Writing a Résumé or Fact Sheet

Use a computer or a typewriter or a computer program specifically designed for résumé composition to set up the information about yourself. Refer to the example on page 162 as a guideline. The information should fit on one page. Make sure that all the information is complete and accurate. Include as much detail as you can about your experiences, especially about the skills you demonstrated. Use interesting but brief sentences to describe them. Finally, read carefully what you have written to make sure it flows well and has no spelling mistakes.

 You might wish to file your résumé or fact sheet in your portfolio.

Laura Chen
164 Blain Road
Anytown, Manitoba
xxx-xxx-xxxx

Objective: Volunteer placement working with animals.

Availability: After school (4:00 to 6:00)

Education: Grade 8
Pleasant Valley School
Anytown, Manitoba

Relevant Experiences: Walk neighbour's dog every morning.
Responsible for care of two pet parakeets.

Skills Demonstrated: Responsible, reliable, experienced with, and
knowledgeable about, a variety of animals.

Relevant Interests: Collect *Peterson Field Guides*.

Memberships: Member of Pleasant Valley Senior School
Reforestation Project.

Member of Manitoba Young Naturalists' Society.

Certificates: St. John Ambulance, Junior First Aid (1996)
Red Cross, Bronze Medallion (1996)

Character References: Pearl Bond (neighbour)
xxx-xxx-xxxx
Max Sands (Science teacher)
xxx-xxx-xxxx

Personal Profile

As well as facts, it is a good idea to give other information about yourself when applying for a position. Consider these questions, for example:
• What is important to you?
• What are your personality strengths?
• What are your skills and aptitudes?
• Where do you want to work?
• What kind of work interests you?

You could write a letter that responds to these questions or you could create a **personal profile** like the one that follows.

Personal Profile

Interests

My favourite subjects in school are: *language arts, French, and art history.*

My academic strengths are: *language arts, art history, science.*

I like to collect: *photographs, illustrations from magazines, postcards, interesting objects.*

The clubs/organizations/teams I belong to are: *The Social Committee, The Yearbook Committee, The Drama Club.*

I have helped my peers in the following ways (List reading buddy, mentoring, peer tutoring experiences): *I have helped a peer get through the novels for his language arts course.*

Three things I know a lot about are: *artists, books, music.*

I have received the following awards: *Best Yearbook Design Award.*

Values

The most important thing in my life is: *being close to my family and having good friends.*

The three values that guide my life are: *honesty, dependability, creativity.*

I really care about: *finding a career that suits my interests.*

Three words that describe me are: *optimistic, honest, open-minded.*

The Future

My dream is to: *become a famous writer.*

Two things that I want to accomplish by the time I am 25 are: *achieve a master's degree in English and publish a novel.*

The areas of work that I am striving towards are: *communications and design.*

Activity 6

Creating a Personal Profile

Consider the statements given in the profile outline you just read. Then create a personal profile about yourself.

 You might wish to file your profile in your portfolio.

Looking Back

1. Which of the self-reflection methods introduced in this chapter do you prefer? Why?

2. In your opinion, what are the skills you now have that will be of most value ten years from now? Why?

EXPLORATIONS

Reflections

Reflect on the message in the statement "I can because I think I can." In what ways have you surprised yourself about what you can do since this course began?

Goals

Look over the categories made by your class-mates in the Imagine Me . . . Imagine You activity bulletin board display. How does your chosen category compare with the choices of others in your class? How many people chose the same quadrant as you did? In what ways are their goals similar to yours? Which quadrant was the most popular? Why? How did this activity help you to focus on your goals?

Action!

Create scenarios in which you are an employer telling young students what they need to do to become successful employees in the future. Use a variety of jobs in your scenarios.

Featuring. . .

Editorial: Write an editorial about the importance of preparing young people now for the Canada of the future.

Advice Column: Write a letter of advice to someone who is preparing for an interview or job-shadowing experience.

Advertisement: Create an advertisement for a workshop at which attendees will have an opportunity to write their personal profile and discuss the steps to getting a community placement.

Personal Story/Interview: Write a description of yourself based on the information gained when you did The Top Ten on page 153.

Research: Put the names of all your classmates in a hat. Draw ten names (a random sample). Collate and compare their results from Imagining Me and You in a Career, page 159. Publish the results, without names, in order to illustrate trends in your class.

Establishing a Route

Now that you know more about your community and how you fit into it, you will have an opportunity to discover the similarities between school and the workplace. You will compare safety at school and on the job. You will see how the skills that increase your success at school can also be applied to work. Finally, you will learn how to select pieces from your portfolio for conferences and evaluations.

Skills for Success in School

What You Will Learn

- To take personal responsibility for your success at school.
- To improve your study habits.
- To manage your time more effectively.
- To resist peer pressure when it affects your school performance.

Terms to Remember

responsibility   time management
self-evaluation   peer pressure
personal work area

The skills you use to succeed at school can often be applied at the workplace and in your personal life as well. It is up to you to become an active learner and to improve areas in your school life that are less than satisfactory. How you see yourself plays an important role in achieving these goals. If you see yourself in a positive way, you can face challenges with more confidence. Evaluating yourself and identifying your problem areas are good starting points. In this chapter, you will evaluate your study habits, your time management, and how you deal with peer pressure. You will also be given suggestions for what to do if you are having difficulty in any of these areas.

Success in School

By the time you graduate from high school, you will have spent approximately ten thousand hours in the classroom. During these hours, your identity, self-esteem, values, career direction, and academic abilities are shaped. As you progress through the grades, you gradually take more **responsibility** for what happens to you at school. You currently play a number of roles: son or daughter, friend, sister or brother, basketball player, reading mentor. Your role as a student will have a major impact on your future.

Activity 1

Reflecting on Yourself as a Learner

What is your picture of yourself as a learner in the classroom? Reflect on this question by completing the following chart.

On a sheet of paper, write the numbers from one to ten. Beside each number, write the number from the scale from one to five that best represents how you see yourself.

How I Feel About Myself as a Learner						
1. successful	1	2	3	4	5	unsuccessful
2. satisfied	1	2	3	4	5	unsatisfied
3. confident	1	2	3	4	5	hesitant
4. better than others	1	2	3	4	5	worse than others
5. stimulated	1	2	3	4	5	bored
6. do my best	1	2	3	4	5	do not do my best
7. good study skills	1	2	3	4	5	poor study skills
8. strong test-taker	1	2	3	4	5	weak test-taker
9. use time well	1	2	3	4	5	waste time
10. good relationships	1	2	3	4	5	weak relationships

When you have finished, pair up. Discuss the following questions.

- How do you see yourself as a learner?
- How do you think you got this picture of yourself?
- How would you like to change? (optional)
- How much does the approval of others (parents/guardians, friends, teachers) affect you?

JOURNAL

Reflecting on Your Sharing

In your journal, record the observations made about you during the discussion with your partner. Then write about how you felt when you shared your questionnaire. Were there any surprising differences between your questionnaires? Complete the following sentence starters in your journal.

When I shared the information with my partner, I felt . . .

It surprised me that my partner's questionnaire . . .

The one major difference in results that my partner and I noticed was . . .

Skill Areas for Classroom Success

If you are going to take responsibility for your learning in the classroom, there are important things you can do to ensure that you are making the best use of your time there.

1. Go to every class and get there on time.

2. Take a notebook, textbooks, planner or organizer, and other required materials to class and be sure to copy down important notes and assignments. Record any homework assignments before you leave the classroom.

3. Take careful notes. Details matter. You might not remember later. Underline or highlight important points.

4. Listen carefully. Respond to questions. Sit near the front if you are easily distracted.

5. Ask questions if you need information or clarification on an issue. Ask for extra help after school if you need it.

6. Participate actively in class. Share your views. Be positive.

7. Find someone (a study buddy) in each class who will agree to share information with you and pass on homework assignments if you are absent. Get your study buddy's phone number.

8. Complete your homework each day.

Activity ②

Using a Self-Evaluation Checklist

Now that you know how to use class time more effectively, complete the following **self-evaluation** checklist at the end of the week. Try to make it a Friday habit. Do it every week and act on the results.

Classroom Success Checklist

These are the elements that are important for doing well in class, and a rating scale for your self-evaluation. Read each sentence in the check-list. On a sheet of paper, write down the number from the rating scale that is most like you for each sentence.

1 = did very well
2 = did well
3 = did OK
4 = some improvement needed
5 = a great deal of improvement needed

1. I have gone to every class on time.
2. I have taken a notebook to every class.
3. I have taken complete notes.
4. I have listened carefully.
5. I have asked questions as needed.
6. I have participated actively.
7. I have a study buddy in each class.
8. I have done my homework.

Evaluating Your Checklist

Study the results of your checklist. Complete the following sentence starters on a sheet of paper.

When I respond to the questions I feel . . .
After three weeks, my score on the checklist is improving because . . .
The one thing that I still need to work on is . . .
I am most proud of the fact that I now . . .

Ideas for Study Success at Home

Another key to success at school is creating a **personal work area** at home. It might be a desk, a table, a comfortable chair, or your bed. Whatever and wherever it is, it should be the type of environment that works best for you. If possible, and with permission, make the space your own by having a calendar or your planner (for due dates and to check things off when completed), dictionary, calculator, paper, pens, and pencils. Go to your work area on a regular basis to do your homework. Then follow the guidelines in the Homework Game to develop good study habits.

The Homework Game

START	SCHOOL	I write down homework in my planner as soon as it is assigned.	I make sure I understand the homework before I leave school.
I reflect on my work. How could I do better? How will I use this learning?			
I hand in my assignments on time.			I ask my teacher for help when I do not understand.
My homework is packed by the door, ready for me to take to school.			I have a study buddy I can phone if I am away from school or if I do not fully understand an assignment.
I keep my notebooks, folders, and portfolios well organized.			HOME
I look after myself and take breaks when I need them.	I do my homework early in the evening before I am too tired.	I avoid distractions like phone calls, television, or the stereo.	I have a quiet place to work.

Developed by the Scarborough Board of Education.

JOURNAL

Planning Your Private Space

Draw a plan for the ideal personal work area and any special features you want it to have. Include the perfect conditions that should exist for you to do your homework. Be as creative as you like. Money, space, and time are no object!

Where Is Your Time Going?

Using a chart similar to this one, keep track of your time for a week. Your total might not add up to 24 hours exactly, but try to be as accurate as you can.

ACTIVITY	SUN.	MON.	TUES.	WED.	THURS.	FRI.	SAT.
Sleep	8	8	8	8	8	8	8
Travel to/from school	0	1	1	1	1	1	0
School classes	0	6	6	6	6	6	0
School clubs, teams	1	0	0	1	0	1	0
Homework	0	1	1	1	1	0	1
Volunteer work, jobs	$\frac{1}{2}$	0	1	0	1	0	1
Household chores	0	$\frac{1}{2}$	$\frac{1}{2}$	$\frac{1}{2}$	$\frac{1}{2}$	$\frac{1}{2}$	$\frac{1}{2}$
Eating	$1\frac{1}{4}$	$1\frac{1}{4}$	$1\frac{1}{4}$	$1\frac{1}{4}$	$1\frac{1}{4}$	$1\frac{1}{4}$	$1\frac{1}{4}$
Dressing	$\frac{1}{2}$	$\frac{1}{4}$	$\frac{1}{2}$	$\frac{1}{4}$	$\frac{1}{2}$	$\frac{1}{4}$	$\frac{1}{2}$
Hobbies/interests	3	1	1	1	1	1	3
Sports	1	$\frac{1}{2}$	0	$\frac{1}{2}$	$\frac{1}{2}$	0	1
Telephone calls	$\frac{1}{4}$	0	0	$\frac{1}{4}$	$\frac{1}{4}$	$\frac{1}{4}$	$\frac{1}{2}$
Watching TV/videos	3	1	1	2	1	1	3
Listening to radio/music	1	$\frac{1}{2}$	$\frac{1}{2}$	$\frac{1}{2}$	$\frac{1}{2}$	1	1
Other (specify)	2						
Total hours	$21\frac{1}{2}$/24	21/24	21/24	$23\frac{1}{4}$/24	$22\frac{1}{2}$/24	$21\frac{1}{4}$/24	$20\frac{3}{4}$/24

1. Look over your chart and write a summary of how you spend your time. Some of the questions to consider while you are writing are:
   • Where is most of your time spent?
   • How is most of your time spent?
   • In which areas can you save time?

2. Choose one category; for example, sleeping or eating. Compare your results in that area with five other people. What did you learn about yourself by making the comparison? Are you planning to try to make any changes in any of the categories?

Activity 3

Managing Your Time

If you think you need help with the way you spend your time, or **time management**, here are some questions to guide your reflections and your decisions for change:
• Do you spend too much time doing certain things?
• In what ways do you waste time?
• What is a problem area for you in managing your time?
• Do you postpone doing important things? Why?
• Do you have difficulty fitting everything into your day? Why?

Identify the areas where you could trim some time and where you need more time. Set a goal to change at least one area at a time. Keep track of your goal and your results.

Peer Pressure

Peer pressure is a term that we hear quite often these days, especially in reference to preteen and teenage students. It has to do with feeling obligated to follow the wishes of your peers in spite of your own wishes.

IN THE NEWS

Growing Pains

by Louise Brown

Children are shaped as much by their peers and their genes as they are by the home, so society should get off parents' backs. This bold claim by sociologist Anne-Marie Ambert, a professor at York University, flies in the face of popular pro-nurture theory, which places the burden of raising happy kids squarely on parents' shoulders.

Yet when Ambert asked 1400 undergraduates between 1974 and 1989 to write about what had made them most happy and unhappy as they grew up, parents were mentioned in not even one-third of these memories. Instead, peers played the leading role, especially in negative memories.

"By far the most common unhappy recollections were of abuse inflicted by their peers, yet parents are the ones who always get blamed (when kids are unhappy)," said Ambert at a parenting conference.

More than half of Ambert's students wrote about how incidents of "peer abuse" had made an impact on their lives. They traced ailments such as ulcers or personality traits such as shyness and self-consciousness to being abused by a peer, verbally, emotionally, or even physically. Surprisingly, very few pinned such problems on parents.

"Don't get me wrong. Parents are a key influence, usually for the good, but these essays suggest it's not parents who play a role in the most pronounced happy or painful memories of childhood. It's peers. I believe society definitely puts too much blame on parents (for problems with children). Kids can get abused by peers and suffer a lot of stress, but they won't tell their parents. Then the kids end up with ulcers, the parents don't know why, and in the end the parents get blamed!"

Even when kids beat each other up, as seems a growing problem in some schools, people ask what the parent did to create the bully or create the victim, says Ambert, "rather than asking the better question: 'What is it about our society that fosters this climate of violence in the first place?'"

Ambert believes a "good home atmosphere is very important.

I'm not arguing that but I'm saying it suddenly can be changed by peers. The peer group itself has an effect that may be more powerful than parents. A great proportion of minor delinquents come from average families. I'm suggesting that maybe parents don't have the power to make or break a child. They are made or broken by other children."

I'm not sure I'm convinced parents play this minor a role. Surely one reason Ambert's students rated parents so low in importance is simply a function of their age. University is a time when young people make their first big break from their parents and they almost need to downplay their parents' importance as part of growing up. It's an age when many of us can recall dismissing our parents' importance as minor—a view we later revise.

Still, Ambert makes an important point: that the whole focus of science has been "How do parents affect their kids?" which neglects other important factors in child development, such as the role of peers and the child's own temperament.

"We have inherited an entire psychological culture, starting with Freud, that sees the child as moulded by the parent, as a clean slate to which the parent adds. How the child turns out is supposed to be entirely the responsibility of the parent. Yet new research suggests the child is co-producer of his or her own development, that children are born with personalities in the making."

Some parents have told Ambert they find the thought of peer influence frightening, but she argues it should be comforting to realize we parents aren't as responsible for our kids' happiness as we had thought. It takes the load off, in a way. We may not be able to guarantee them happiness, but nor can we singlehandedly spoil things for them, either.

Reprinted by permission of Louise Brown.

1. Discuss whether or not you agree that children are shaped as much by their peers and their own temperament as they are by their parents.

2. Write about an incident when you were strongly influenced by peers. Why were you influenced? Was it a positive or a negative influence? What would you do the next time? How can you be sure?

Activity **4** •

Role-Playing Difficult Situations

With a partner, create conversations using two of these situations as the starting point. Then create two of your own, based on your experiences.

• A few minutes before math class, a friend asks you to give her your homework to copy.

• As you are leaving school, some friends from another class invite you to play basketball. You have a science test and a book report due; they do not.

• Your older brother offers you one of his English essays in exchange for cleaning up the kitchen for him.

• Your best friend wants to be your partner on a project. The last time you worked together, you did a second-rate job.

• Just as you start reviewing for a math quiz, your best friend from camp makes a surprise visit.

Responding to the Role-Play

Even though you were only role-playing difficult peer situations, real feelings might have been aroused. Respond to the following:

• When I think about responding to a friend in a negative way, I . . .

• Even though I was only role-playing in an activity, I felt . . .

Activity 5

Describing Expectations

In a chart like the following, write on the arrows at least five expectations you feel people have of you. Consider those that can be met and those that will take a long time (or can never be met), and decide on their priority by numbering your statements in the circles provided. Then make a personal comment about each expectation. For each item, consider a plan of specific actions you could take to meet or deal with these expectations.

Expectations

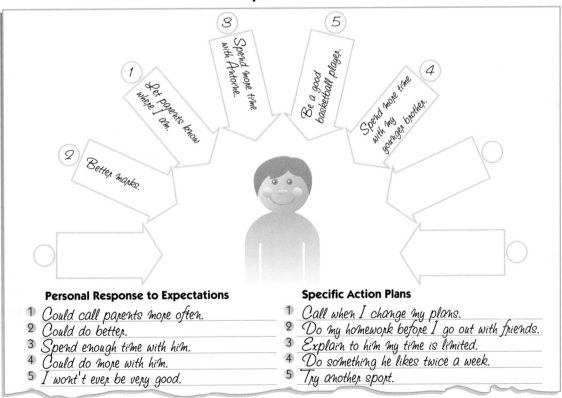

Personal Response to Expectations	**Specific Action Plans**
1 Could call parents more often.	1 Call when I change my plans.
2 Could do better.	2 Do my homework before I go out with friends.
3 Spend enough time with him.	3 Explain to him my time is limited.
4 Could do more with him.	4 Do something he likes twice a week.
5 I won't ever be very good.	5 Try another sport.

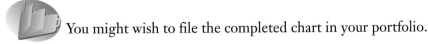

You might wish to file the completed chart in your portfolio.

Looking Back

1. Which of the chapter activities will help you to take responsibility for your own success in the classroom? In what ways will they help you?

2. What are two benefits of managing your time?

3. Peer pressure often interferes with school success. Discuss this idea in terms of your own experience.

EXPLORATIONS

Reflections

Saying no to your peers is difficult. For each of the following statements, outline a situation when you might say:
- No, thanks.
- That's not for me.
- I'd rather not.
- You've got to be kidding.
- Sorry, not now.

You might wish to draw the scenario or create a cartoon strip or a storyboard.

Goals

Think of a short-term goal that you have achieved recently. How many steps did you have to take? Which was the most difficult? How did you feel when you achieved your goal?

Action!

Use one of the statements from the Reflections activity in a skit in which a friend is trying to influence you in a negative way.

Featuring. . .

Editorial: You are the editor of your school newspaper. You are graduating to another school and leaving your readership of three years. Write an inspirational editorial about the value of the effort you have spent in the position of editor.

Advice Column: Write a letter advising a peer to try to improve his or her school attendance. Include suggestions on how to get up and get to school, as well as the benefits of regular attendance.

Advertisement: Prepare an advertisement to attract students from another province to attend your school as a part of an exchange program. Your advertisement should contain a variety of features, available at your school and in your community, which will appeal to a wide audience.

Research: Survey fellow students to find out their homework habits. Include the categories of time, duration, location, and rewards. Graph the results.

Personal Story/Interview: Ask several students to share their journal entry about their ideal private space, on page 171. Write an article reporting on the one that is both practical and creative.

Skills for Success in the Workplace

What You Will Learn

- How attending school prepares you for the workplace.
- Some of the knowledge, skills, and attitudes needed in the workplace.
- How to communicate effectively.
- Safety factors in the workplace.

Terms to Remember

traffic flow   paraphrase

initiative   certification

communication

School and the workplace have many things in common. The interiors and landscapes of both environments are planned so that people's activities can be carried out in an organized and productive manner. The subjects you learn at school are applied in real situations on the job. Social skills, such as initiating, co-operating, and communicating, are an asset wherever you are. Many health and safety practices learned at school are valuable and necessary for the workplace. This chapter will focus on comparisons between school and the workplace and on the knowledge and skills that are applicable to both.

School and the Workplace

The physical structures of school and the workplace have similarities. Both are designed to provide spaces for the activities that take place there. The plans also take into account the **traffic flow**—the number of people that will need to be accommodated in the hallways—the equipment and furnishings needed, and other features that will make people comfortable, such as windows, drinking fountains, a cafeteria or vending machines, and washrooms. Much of the information and many of the skills you learn at school are also applied by workers at their jobs. The following activities will help you make a more detailed comparison between school and work.

Activity 1

Comparing Environments

Choose a workplace with which you are familiar or one about which you can get facts or make observations. Compare it to your school in a chart similar to the following.

Comparing School and a Workplace

	SCHOOL	WORKPLACE
Name of Building		
Building Size		
Conveniences for Users		
Inside Organization/Use		
Outside Organization/Use		
Inside Traffic Patterns		
Outside Traffic Patterns		
Number of Daily Users		
Hours of Operation		

In Chapter 12, you looked at the skills you have that can be used in the workplace. Since your future career is probably not yet decided, it is a good idea to take the major subjects at school so that you can change your mind later if you wish. The following chart demonstrates the skills you learn at school in courses and activities and how the same skills can be used in the workplace.

Building Your Work Skills in School

SCHOOL SKILLS	COURSES AND ACTIVITIES THAT BUILD THESE SKILLS	HOW THESE SKILLS WILL HELP YOU IN THE WORKPLACE
Communication Skills • Giving class presentations • Reading articles and books • Writing essays, short stories, and poetry 	Language Arts Languages Social Studies Art Student Council School Newspaper	• Prepare presentations • Write clear and concise memos, letters, and reports • Speak well on issues • Explain your ideas effectively • Ask for help when required
Teamwork Skills • Getting along with your classmates • Working with others on projects 	Social Studies Science Physical Education Trades and Technology Music Student Council Clubs Sports Teams School Band/Orchestra	• Be a productive team worker • Accept supervision • View co-workers as equals • Know how to be co-operative and share knowledge
Time Management Skills • Doing homework • Meeting project deadlines • Scheduling your day • Getting to class on time	All courses and activities 	• Get work done efficiently • Be prepared for meetings • Meet deadlines • Plan schedules and set goals
Problem-Solving Skills • Analyzing information • Understanding the problem • Defining the problem • Solving the problem • Applying the results 	Science Math Business Social Studies Trades and Technology Student Council	• Think analytically and clearly about issues • Pinpoint problems • Evaluate situations • Identify risks • Make informed decisions • Find productive solutions

Organizational Skills

- Taking notes
- Following written and oral instructions
- Keeping binders of information
- Following a schedule
- Setting priorities and goals

All courses and activities

- Keep a neat workplace
- Take care of equipment and tools
- Keep track of important details
- Handle interruptions well
- Organize activities to meet deadlines

Learning Skills

- Asking questions
- Reading information
- Using the library
- Researching information
- Joining activities and clubs
- Trying new things
- Meeting new people

All courses and activities

- Think critically and act logically
- Learn from on-the-job training
- Upgrade skills as necessary
- Learn from mistakes
- Increase knowledge and productivity

Computer Skills

- Learning storyboard
- Learning word processing
- Learning database programs

Math
Science
Business
Trades and Technology
Computer Studies

- Be computer literate
- Use technology in the workplace
- Adapt to new technologies

Listening Skills

- Attending classes
- Going to lectures
- Taking notes
- Visualizing what you hear
- Comprehending information

All courses and activities

"I get it!"

- Understand what managers and co-workers tell you
- Help others with their concerns
- Participate effectively in meetings

Creativity Skills

- Learning how others have been creative
- Using your imagination
- Trying new ways to do things
- Looking at issues from a different point of view

Language Arts
Art
Music
Science
Drama Club
School Band/Orchestra

- Be an idea person
- Think of new ways to get the job done
- Create a positive work environment
- Increase motivation

Leadership Skills

- Leading projects
- Being on sports teams
- Volunteering as a peer helper

Science
History
Music
Physical Education
School Activities

- Lead projects
- Manage projects
- Coach others
- Help others reach their goals

Activity ②

Applying School Subjects to the Workplace

This activity focusses on the subjects you are taught at school and how they are used by specific workers. Create a chart like the following sample, and give examples for Mathematics, Language Arts, Science, Health/Physical Education, Technology, and History/Geography.

SUBJECT	SAMPLE JOBS	HOW SUBJECT IS USED
Mathematics	Plumber	• Computes measurements. • Reads plans. • Understands scaled drawings.
	Travel Agent	• Computes discounts, taxes. • Compares prices.
	Language Arts Teacher	• Computes students' marks.
Language Arts	Carpenter	• Reads trade journals to follow new product development.

PORTFOLIO

Reflecting on the School-Work Connection

Complete the following sentences on a sheet of paper.

After completing the chart, I'm beginning to wonder . . .

I think I have changed my opinion about . . .

As I work on these subjects at school, I hope that . . .

Initiative at School and in the Workplace

Initiative means doing what should be done without being told to do it. When you initiate something, it means you start it. Someone who comes up with new ideas, who solves small problems without looking for help or direction, and who can be trusted to work on his or her own is showing initiative. This person will probably do better work and enjoy the job more than someone who must be directed all the time. The chart on page 184 illustrates the similarities.

PROFILE

Two Honoured for Building Racial Harmony

by Debra Black

Abhi Ahluwalia and Trudy-Ann (Debbie) Young believe they can change the world. In their own way, they have already begun to make a difference and help build racial harmony and eliminate discrimination in Ontario.

The pair, recipients of the 1997 Lincoln M. Alexander Awards, were honoured yesterday at a ceremony at Queen's Park in Toronto with both Lieutenant-Governor Hilary Weston and former lieutenant-governor Alexander attending.

"In their determination to promote equality and awareness, these two young people have demonstrated exemplary leadership and commitment," said Alexander, who presented the awards. The ceremony was one of many activities marking the United Nation's International Day for the Elimination of Racial Discrimination.

"This is just the beginning," 23-year-old Ahluwalia said in an interview. "There's lots of work to be done . . . . They say youth are the leaders of tomorrow. I think youth are the leaders of today."

Ahluwalia was nominated for his efforts as a volunteer with the Race Relations Committee of Kitchener-Waterloo. He also has organized three major youth conferences on anti-discrimination, founded a clothing company that features products with anti-discrimination messages, and done work in conflict resolution training.

Trudy-Ann Young is a 19-year-old student at Jarvis Collegiate Institute in Toronto. She believes a lot of work remains to be done if true equality is going to be achieved. But she believes her generation has the tools to make that happen.

"There is a stereotype that this generation, my generation, is apathetic," said Young, who plans to study sociology and English at McGill University. "But we're not. We're very politicized. I think it's important to point out there are a lot

Trudy-Ann (Debbie) Young and Abhi Ahluwalia with Lieutenant-Governor Hilary Weston and Lincoln Alexander.

of young people out there doing what we're doing. I work with all kinds of exemplary youth. I see their drive and passion."

Young won her award for her efforts to deal with racism and discrimination. She is the editor of *The Jarvis Jargon*, which was selected as the best school newspaper by *The Toronto Star*. She also co-ordinated a school-wide Black History Month, hosts and produces a talk show for young people on CKLN radio, is president of the African History Club, and has led anti-racism youth training groups.

1. List the projects that Young and Ahluwalia initiated. Beside each activity, indicate who would be influenced by it.

2. Ahluwalia says, "They say youth are the leaders of tomorrow. I think youth are the leaders of today." Look around your school community. In what ways do you see youth living up to this statement?

3. Young says that "there are a lot of young people out there doing what we're doing." What evidence do you see?

4. If you could recommend someone in your school for this award, who would it be? Why?

Initiative at School and in the Workplace

AT SCHOOL	IN THE WORKPLACE
• Participates in class.	• Shows a willingness to work.
• Does work as assigned.	• Is busy with assigned tasks.
• Welcomes extra work.	• Does extra work as required.
• Meets after school for projects.	• Works overtime if required.
• Is a mentor for a reading buddy.	• Helps others with work if required.
• Suggests alternatives in group work.	• Presents better ways to get a job done.
• Takes certification courses.	• Takes extra courses to improve performance.
• Understands time management.	• Meets time lines and is prompt.

Activity 3

Taking the Initiative at School

One of the ways that you and your classmates can show initiative is to plan an event or activity to help another class or group in your school community.

1. Brainstorm some ideas.

2. Ask these questions about each idea:
   • Is it practical?
   • Is it fun?

- Will it help?
- Do we have enough time to do it?
- What help do we need?

3. Make a chart to compare the ideas.

Decision-Making	Is it practical?	Is it fun?	Will it help?	Do we have time?	Who can help?
Idea 1					

4. Make a decision based on the criteria.

5. Begin the planning of the group's choice. Use an organizer to help you.

Things We Will Need	Steps to Success	Possible Problems	Solutions

Reflecting on Opportunities to Show Initiative

Complete the following sentences in your journal.

When I am in situations in which I have opportunities to show initiative, I must remember . . .

It is important for me to . . .

When I am part of a project planning team, I . . .

Interacting with Others

In most school activities, you do not work alone. The same is true in the workplace. You are expected to work well with your co-workers, just as you are expected to work well with your classmates, in order to be as productive as possible. Because you cannot change other people, you need to be aware of your attitude, or way of thinking, acting, or feeling, in order to get along with them.

Activity 4

Assessing Your Attitude

Think about how you feel toward people with whom you come in contact at school. Ask yourself the following questions, then, on a sheet of paper, write a "yes" or "no" for your answer beside each question number.

1. Are you able to separate what the person says and does from who the person is?

2. Do you try to understand why a person is behaving in a certain way?

3. Do you look for the positive qualities in a person, to balance the things you do not like about him or her?

4. Are you aware of how your own attitude and feelings might be affecting your behaviour toward others?

If you answered "yes" to most of the questions, you are on the way to being a productive worker. You have a choice: you can react positively or negatively to other people.

JOURNAL

Reflecting on Your Interactions

Complete the following sentences in your journal.

I interact poorly with others when . . .
I enjoy interacting with others when . . .
To keep myself focussed on a person's positive qualities, I . . .
I also try to improve my interaction with others by . . .

The Art of Communicating

Listening

Many of the problems that occur at home, school, and in the workplace are a result of poor **communication**. To communicate, you must listen to others as well as make sure that you are clearly understood.

Activity 5

Rating Your Listening Skills

It is said that careful listening is a habit. Rate your listening habits. On a sheet of paper, write the number from the scale that best represents how you act in each of the twelve situations.

Are You a Good Listener?

1-Usually   2-Often   3-Sometimes   4-Not usually   5-Hardly ever

1. After only a short period of listening, you start thinking about what you are going to say next.
2. If you do not like the person, you do not really listen to what he or she is saying.
3. You interrupt others before they have finished talking.
4. You pretend to pay attention.
5. You usually talk about yourself.
6. You seldom ask questions.
7. You don't give other people a chance to talk.
8. You don't see things from the other person's point of view.
9. You avoid eye contact when listening.
10. You get so busy taking notes that you miss some of what is said.
11. You get distracted easily.
12. You let your mind wander or you daydream when someone else is talking.

Add the numbers to get your score.
• If you scored 45-60, you are a good listener, and probably make few mistakes in your work. People enjoy talking to you and being with you.
• If you scored 31-44, you need to improve your listening skills. This will also improve your performance.
• If you scored 12-30, you do not listen well.

Paraphrasing

One way to improve communication is to **paraphrase**. Paraphrasing means repeating what a person has said to you in your own words. It establishes whether you understood the message as it was intended. For example:

Activity 6

Paraphrasing Your Partner's Statements

Read the five statements below. With a partner, take turns paraphrasing the statements.

1. I don't like the work I'm doing on this. It just doesn't seem to be right.

2. It bugs me that my mother wears that hat.

3. This work table is a mess!

4. I wish that we could do something else.

5. It seems like the summer is going to be very long for us.

Safety in the Workplace

Safety in the workplace should be a concern of all young employees, since statistics have shown that they are the ones at most risk. You can prepare yourself for being safe by observing and understanding the reasons for safety features at home and at school, and by taking training courses.

Activity 7

Looking for Signs of School Safety

Look around your school for signs of safety. The following chart offers ideas for some observations you might make.

ITEM OR SIGN	LOCATION	REASON FOR CONCERN
Wet Floor sign	Inside door to school yard	Wet floors are slippery
In/Out signs on doors	Into school yard	People could collide
Eyewash station	Science room	Chemicals burn eyes
Goggles	Wood shop	Flying splinters

Record your examples as you see them, then present the information visually in a bulletin board display or a mural, using drawings or pictures of the items, their location, and the reasons for concern.

IN THE NEWS

Serious Safety

Eager to make a good impression at a new job, we might not want to bother the boss by asking about safety training. But we wouldn't play our favourite sports without the proper training and equipment, so why ignore safety at work? After working hard for our opportunities, it's important not to let a workplace injury turn a dream job into a nightmare. Accidents can happen in any industry. Workplace hazards can include spills, contamination, and equipment. Statistics show that most workplace injuries happen within the first two weeks of employment and workers under the age of 24 have the greatest risk for injury or death.

"Safety is one of the most important things you can learn on the job," says Beryl Kirk of Human Resources Development Canada, the federal agency responsible for the Canada Labour Code. "In school you studied hard and as a result landed your first job. Now learning to do it safely may help you keep it."

At age 21, Mel Camilli lost both his legs in a logging truck accident. Now an employee with the Workers' Compensation Board of British Columbia, he urges people to be aware of hazards, ask safety questions, and report dangerous situations to help prevent occupational accidents. "It's a hard thing to do as a young person. You never think anything bad is going to happen to you," he says. "But don't be afraid to ask questions. The boss is there to help and is not going to fire you for asking."

Under the Canada Labour Code you have the right to a safe workplace, training, proper equipment and practices, and to refuse to do unsafe work. It's important to recognize risky situations in your work environment and find out how to avoid them. "Insist on training," says Bryan Collett, Education-Outreach Co-ordinator with Workers' Compensation Board. "Lack of experience in the workforce and lack of training can put workers at risk."

Almost every accident is preventable with the right training, procedures, and gear. When starting a new job, take some time to talk about safety. Ask about hazards, training, procedures, and first aid. Get familiar with the site and equipment and learn to recognize dangerous situations.

This landscaper is wearing protective gloves, ear muffs, and a hard hat with a visor.

Reprinted with permission from *Career Paths* 1996, published by YES Canada-BC and funded by Human Resources Development Canada and the BC Ministry of Education, Skills and Training.

1. Why should safety knowledge be a priority with new employees?

2. Contact your local Workers' Compensation Board and ask them to send you materials on workplace safety.

3. Make safety posters for your school. Focus on potential hazards in and around your school building.

Certification Courses

You can extend your health and safety knowledge by participating in a training or **certification** course offered by many local organizations, such as:

• Cardiopulmonary Resuscitation (CPR)
• First aid courses (sponsored by St. John Ambulance)
• Red Cross swimming qualifications
• Workplace Hazardous Materials Information Systems (WHMIS) workplace safety

When you can add these courses to your résumé or fact sheet, or add the certificates from them to your fact folder, it indicates that you are a responsible individual who is interested in planning now for the future.

CASE STUDY

Pair Honoured for Bravery in Saving Drowning Boy

By Debora Van Brenk

Perry Wardle and Stacy Coxon.

The Blenheim, Ontario, public pool was crowded with children. Kids on the deck, kids in the water, kids swimming laps, kids playing games. Only 11-year-old swimmer Perry Wardle noticed a small figure floating, face-down and motionless, beneath the surface in the deep end of the pool. He raced to the boy, dove under water, and pulled the child to the side of the pool and to safety.

Wardle, now 13, was among several civilians from Southwestern Ontario who were honoured by provincial police at a heroes' luncheon.

"I was scared but I just tried to remember what I was taught in lifesaving," said Wardle, who is working on his bronze medallion in swimming and is on the Blenheim swim team.

Wardle's swim coach, Stacy Coxon, was lifeguard that summer's day in 1995 and carried the boy from the pool after Wardle's heroics. When she noticed the five-year-old wasn't breathing, she did mouth-to-mouth resuscitation. He still wasn't breathing. She managed to dislodge from the boy's throat some gum he had been chewing and he began to breathe again.

Within five minutes, the boy was back to his normal self. "He has these huge brown eyes and he just looked up at me," recalled Coxon.

The rescue was, she said, part of her job. But it was more than that, too. "I've made the biggest difference that anyone can make by saving a life."

1. Write a letter from the boy's mother to Perry and Stacy.

2. Retell the story from the point of view of the boy who was rescued.

3. Write a newspaper article that could have appeared on the day of the rescue.

Looking Back

1. Create a questionnaire, based on your knowledge of the connection between school and work skills, which would be given to employers so they could rate which school skills they consider to be the most important.

2. Name three workplace skills that you can practise in your daily life.

3. What is your favourite subject at school? List the jobs for which it has importance.

EXPLORATIONS

Reflections

"Today's children are Canada's future." Why do adults often say this? Reflect on how you, as a young person, will affect the future of today's adults as they grow older.

Goals

Outline the steps you would take in the next year to achieve at least one of the certification courses mentioned in this chapter.

Action!

Create skits to perform for younger students in your school. Use ideas from this chapter, such as:
- Getting along with others.
- The results of not listening.
- Planning an event for your class.
- Safety in the school.

Featuring. . .

Editorial: Write an editorial about the importance of planning for the future instead of always concentrating on the present.

Advice Column: Write a letter advising parents how to help their child prepare for the workplace of the future.

Advertisement: Create an advertisement for the skits created in Action! List the topics available and the steps to follow to book a performance.

Personal Story/Interview: Interview the staff members who clean your school. Ask what steps they must take to ensure your school is a safe place.

Research: Interview three of your neighbours about the safe practices they use at their jobs. Make a list of the safety equipment they use, if applicable. Combine your findings.

Your Career Exploration Portfolio

What You Will Learn

- The purpose and advantages of portfolios.
- How to organize the portfolio items collected.
- How to select portfolio items for evaluation.
- How to share your experiences through conferences.

Terms to Remember

Collect, Select, Reflect model
portfolio conference

What Is a Career Exploration Portfolio?

As you have been adding items to your portfolio, you have seen that a portfolio contains many things in many forms.

- It is filled with reminders of your daily experiences, both in school and in the community, that have helped you develop your academic and interpersonal skills.
- It shows how these experiences have contributed to shaping your career plans.
- It helps you to remember what you have done and to reflect on what you want to accomplish in the future.
- It clarifies your understanding of your interests, abilities, and aspirations.

    A successful portfolio is based on the **Collect, Select, Reflect model.**

- Collect all your items for the portfolio.
- Select the pieces for your final portfolio.
- Reflect on your selections.

The Use of Portfolios

You will understand more about the use of portfolios when you read this letter that one teacher sends home to her students' parents or guardians before students begin their career exploration course each year.

Dear Parent or Guardian,

This term, as a part of our career unit, the students will develop portfolios. The contents of these individual portfolios will reflect what students are learning about themselves, their community and their role in it, and their future careers. Students will choose the contents, guided by the teacher and peers.

   Although the emphasis might be on written materials (journals, interest tests, reports, charts), students will also be encouraged to include photos, recordings of interviews, and other objects that reflect their experiences. There will also be notes that the student and I will make at the regular conferences we will have to discuss the contents of his or her portfolio.

   Please support us in this venture and encourage your child by asking him or her about what he or she is collecting. Remember that this working portfolio is a full collection to promote self-awareness and growth; it is not a tidy show-piece. I hope that you will join us for the final conference when your son or daughter will select materials from the portfolio to present.

   Call me if you have any concerns, questions, or suggestions.

Sincerely,
P. G. Bloom

Activity ❶

Responding to Parents' Concerns

Put yourself in the place of the parent or guardian who is receiving this letter. What concerns, questions, or suggestions might he or she have about the portfolio? What if the parent sees the student as untidy, irresponsible, and always losing things or in need of more guidance in reading, writing, and mathematics? What if the parent thinks that tests and exams are the only way to find out what someone has learned? What if the parent does not understand the purpose behind the portfolio? Create four concerns, questions, or suggestions from a parent's point of view. Write positive responses to them from your point of view. Rewrite these as a telephone dialogue.

What People Say

What a student says

I am having fun collecting a variety of things for my portfolio. It is not difficult to write about my experiences when I know the purpose of my writing. But picture-taking is my favourite activity. I never realized that pictures could tell such stories, and I have some amazing ones!

What a teacher says

The quality of student work after the introduction of portfolios has exceeded my expectations. They enjoy the challenge of gathering a variety of work to illustrate their learning. As well, they have become so much more reflective and aware of their experiences, especially those outside of the classroom.

What a parent says

I appreciate the use of portfolios because they make young people think about what they are doing now and what effect the present has on the future. My son has created a special journal of his participation in community happenings in our town. He will value this forever, and so will I!

What a sponsoring agency says

We have enjoyed watching our student volunteers choose and create items for their portfolios. They are excited about this method of recording and reproducing their experiences.

Activity 2

Responding to What People Say

Read over What People Say. Write a response to one of them in which you tell why you agree or disagree.

Or

Write a similar paragraph titled "What I Say."

Or

Choose three statements with which you agree and tell why you do.

Putting It All Together

Throughout this book, items have been identified and suggested as possible portfolio selections. When you add your own choices to some of these, you will have quite a number of pieces. You will probably need a large storage container. You could choose a unique container, and further personalize it by decorating it. Items for storing portfolio materials could include file folders, photo albums or scrapbooks, envelopes, and video- or audio tapes. You will also need a variety of pens, pencils, markers, paper, art supplies, and recording equipment.

What Do I Put in My Portfolio?

- Evidence of progress toward goals—goals journal, certificates, report cards.
- Items from out-of-classroom experiences—photos, pictures, video- or audio tapes, written reports, articles, or letters.
- Products of activities done with the class—charts, graphs, polls, records of presentations.
- Items that demonstrate accomplishments—badges, certificates, letters of recommendation.
- Items that show skills, interests, and attitudes—personal inventories, photographs.
- Items that tell about the school year—scrapbooks, photo albums, and videotapes.
- Evidence of reflection—journals, evaluation checklists.
- Anything you want!

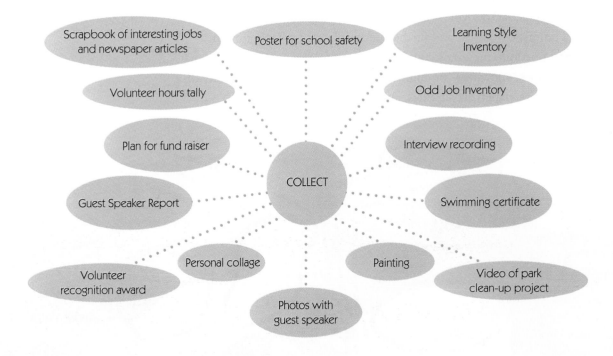

Select and Reflect

Take time to look through your portfolio items. Sort the items so that they reflect your knowledge, skills, and attitudes. As you look at the items and try to decide what to select, ask yourself these questions:

- Why did I choose this?
- In what way(s) is it important to me?

- How does it illustrate one of my accomplishments?
- What would I say if I showed it to someone? What do I want that person to know?
- To whom would I like to show it?

When preparing to share portfolio contents in an evaluation conference, select a variety of items that illustrate:

- creativity
- quality
- persistence
- thoughtfulness
- progress
- diversity
- organization
- awareness
- knowledge
- accuracy

Activity 3

Preparing for Sharing

To prepare for sharing, you might want to complete the following sentences for each piece you have selected from your portfolio. It will help you organize your thinking in preparation for speaking.

I have included this piece because . . .
I want you to know that . . .
When I did this I learned . . .
I want to work on improving . . .

Activity 4

Holding a Practice Conference

Before presenting your portfolio to your teacher, you might wish to rehearse with a classmate to become more comfortable with the experience. Participating successfully in a **portfolio conference** requires a great deal of practice. Here is a plan for practising with a classmate.

Person A: Spreads out portfolio items and tells why each has been included.
Person B: Listens and asks relevant questions.
Person A: Responds to questions.
Person B: Listens and makes two or three positive comments or suggestions.
Person A: Thanks person B and offers him or her a comment sheet to complete (optional).
Person B: Completes the sheet.

Setting Up the Portfolio Conference

Having a conference about items from your Career Exploration Portfolio is a
good idea because:
• You get an opportunity to choose and profile your best work.
• More people see and hear about the work you have been doing.
• A variety of media can be used. Evaluation is not just a mark from a test or an exam.
• More than one person can participate.
    In preparation for the conference, ask yourself the following questions:
• What are the goals of the conference?
• Who will be invited?
• When can these people meet?
• How long will it take?
• What preparations will I have to make?

Portfolio Conference Outline

Those who come to your portfolio conference might be more comfortable if
you give them an outline to explain what will happen. For example:
• This work covers the time period from — to — .
• The goals of this conference are . . .
• The purpose of my portfolio is . . .
• The contents will illustrate . . .
• You are welcome to ask questions about . . .

Reflecting on Your Portfolio Conference

Once your portfolio conference has taken place, it would be a good idea to
reflect on the experience and record your thoughts and feelings in your journal
or on a sheet of paper to include in your portfolio. You might want to consider
some of the following sentence starters to guide your reflections.

My Plans

If I could do this over again, I would . . .
I want to know more about . . .
It is important for me . . .
Before I start next time I will . . .
I want to practise . . .
I am going to think about . . .

My Work

I had the most fun . . .
I was nervous about . . .
What is good about this work is . . .
This is my best work because . . .
I wish I had remembered to . . .
I want people who see this work to know . . .

My Learning

I am getting better at . . .
When I did . . . I learned . . .
I know I need help with . . .
I think I did a good job because . . .
What this work tells about me is . . .
My strength in . . . is . . .

Developed by the Scarborough Board of Education.

Looking Back

1. Your portfolio contains a variety of items that reflect what you have learned. Make a list of materials and equipment you would require to create the ultimate portfolio. Cost is no object.

2. Now that you and your peers have participated in portfolio conferences, how would you explain the advantages to younger students?

3. Which article from your portfolio is your favourite? For what reasons?

4. Which item would you like to replace? Why?

5. Make a list of all the items in your portfolio. Categorize them by level of interest, importance, or difficulty.

EXPLORATIONS

Reflections

As your last journal entry, complete the following sentences.

When I first started collecting items for my portfolio I thought . . .
After a while, I began to realize . . .
Now that my portfolio is complete, I feel that I . . .
The time spent on career exploration has made me realize . . .

Goals

When you discuss your own work and listen to the responses from your peers, teachers, and parents or guardians, you are learning about your learning and the achievement of your goals. What two long-term goals are now clear to you? What can you do in the next year to move toward them? What steps will you be taking soon to make them happen?

Action!

Create a series of monologues that reflect the following situations:
- What a student is thinking when choosing items for a portfolio conference.
- What a teacher is thinking during a conference.
- What a parent or guardian is thinking when he or she sees a number of portfolio items but cannot really understand their purpose.

Featuring. . .

Editorial: Write an editorial that offers your opinion on the value of portfolios for students, peers, teachers, and parents or guardians in measuring what was learned.

Advice Column: Create a ten-point checklist and guide to help other students in their creation of an excellent portfolio.

Advertisement: Create an illustrated advertisement for five different containers for portfolio items.

Personal Story/Interview: Develop five questions about the portfolio conference experience. Ask the same questions of the following participants: student, peer, teacher.

Research: Take a poll in the classroom to see which items students chose as most important in their portfolios. Illustrate your findings on a graph.

Photo Credits

page 8 Dick Hemingway; **page 10** Canapress Photo Service; **page 12** *The Toronto Star*/K. Beaty; **page 16** *The Toronto Star*/B. Spremo; **pages 15, 17** Dick Hemingway; **page 18** Canapress Photo Service/ Reed Saxon; **page 19** Canapress Photo Service/Andrew Vaughan; **page 40** Photo by Vendula Ralkova, courtesy of *Career Paths* Newspaper; **page 50** Dick Hemingway; **page 51** Canapress Photo Service; **page 55** *The Toronto Star*/B. Dexter (top left), *The Toronto Star*/J. Mahler (top right), *The Toronto Star*/ A. Munro (bottom left), *The Toronto Star*/S. Russell (bottom right); **page 61** Courtesy of Bronwen Hughes; **page 74** Dick Hemingway (top and bottom left), Sue Ogrocki/Reuters/Archive Photos (top right), Canapress Photo Service (bottom right); **page 82** *The Toronto Sun*/Greig Reekie; **page 93** Reprinted by permission of the Pathfinder Learning Centre, Port au Port West, Newfoundland; **page 96** *The Toronto Star*/P. Irish; **page 99** Bayne Stanley; **page 106** Chris Schwarz/*Maclean's*; **page 108** *The Toronto Star*/ P. Power; **page 109** Reprinted by permission of Sara Beaudry, National Native Role Model Program; **page 111** Peter Bregg/*Maclean's*; **page 113** Photography by Rich Chard; **page 121** Stuart Davis/*The Province*; **page 122** *The Toronto Star*/S. Russell; **page 123** Courtesy of Jenna Huberty; **page 124** Photo by Brant Drewery and reprinted by permission of Frank Ogden; **page 125** Courtesy of Constance Edwards; **page 129** Mike Pinder; **page 132** © Canadian Red Cross (centre), Reprinted by permission of the Ontario Community Support Association (OCSA). OCSA is an organization of more than 300 direct providers of community-based not-for-profit health and social service agencies in Ontario. (bottom); **page 133** Corporation of the City of Oshawa, 1997 (top left and centre), United Way of Canada - Centraide Canada (top right); **page 134** Brian Gavriloff/*Edmonton Journal*; **page 136** Bayne Stanley; **page 143** Mario Pietramala/*Edmonton Journal*; **page 147** *The Toronto Star*/K. Faught; **page 149** © Dan Callis; **page 154** *The Toronto Star*/R. Bull; **page 160** Photo reprinted by permission of The Mammoth Recording Company of Carrboro. Photo by Mark Van-S; **pages 168, 173** Dick Hemingway; **page 183** *The Toronto Star*/R. Lautens; **page 189** Dick Hemingway; **page 190** Debora Van Brenk/*London Free Press*; **page 194** Dick Hemingway

Text Credits

p. 7	"Teenagers' Values Across Canada" From *The Emerging Generation* by Reginald Bibby and Donald Posterski, 1985. Reprinted by permission of Stoddart Publishing Co. Limited.
pp. 20-21, 24-28	"Identifying a Person's Intelligence" and "Learning Styles" Excerpted from *Psychology for Kids* by Jonni Kincher, © 1995, 1990 with permission from Free Spirit Publishing Inc., Minneapolis, MN. Telephone 1-800-735-7323. ALL RIGHTS RESERVED.
pp. 21-23	"Personality Type" True Colors, created by Don Lowry © 1992 and adapted for this book by Diana Ketterman, Ph.D., co-author of ESI's True Colors ClassRunner. True Colors ® is a registered trademark of True Colors Inc. For further information on True Colors and Career Education contact Education Systems International (ESI) at 2875 Sampson Avenue, Corona, CA 91719. Telephone 1-800-422-4686.
p. 40	Reprinted with permission from *Career Paths* 1996, published by YES Canada — BC and funded by Human Resources Development Canada and the BC Ministry of Education, Skills and Training. For more information, Phone: (604) 435-1937, FAX: (604) 435-5548, E-mail: editor@careerpathsonline.com, Website: http://careerpathsonline.com
p. 41	"You're Allowed" From *You're Allowed To Be Happy!* by Barry Davis published by Octopus Publishing Group (NZ) Ltd. ISBN 0-86863-897-8. Reprinted by permission of the author.
p. 46	"What is the best advice a new high school student could receive?" *The Education Forum Magazine: The Magazine for Professional Educators.*

p. 54   "What Is Out There?"
                Adapted from Canada Career Information Partnership, *Canada Prospects* and *Ontario Prospects*, 1996.

p. 65   "Molly McGoo's Exceptionally Great Cookies"
                From *The Money Tree Myth* by Gail Vaz-Oxlade, 1996. Reprinted with the permission of Stoddart Publishing Co. Limited.

p. 68   "Jake's Questions"
                Reprinted from "The Edge" by Human Resources Development Canada.
                Reproduced with the permission of the Minister of Public Works and Government Services Canada, 1997.

p. 68   "Monthly Contribution"
                TD Asset Management Inc.

pp. 75-77   "Career Clusters" and "Playing the Job Trek Game"
                Adapted from Canada Career Information Partnership, *Canada Prospects* and *Ontario Prospects*, Spring 1995.

pp. 77-78   "Creating Job Advertisements"
                Reproduced with the permission of The Bridges Initiatives Inc. Producers of the only online across-the-school career development system. Telephone 1-800-281-1168.

pp. 83-84   "Today's Facts, Tomorrow's Possibilities"
                Adapted from Canada Career Information Partnership, *Canada Prospects* and *Ontario Prospects*, Spring 1995.

pp. 84-85   "New Ways to Work"
                Alberta Advanced Education & Career Development.

p. 87   "Job Trends"
                Adapted from *Where the Jobs Are: Career Survival for Canadians in the New Global Economy* by Colin Campbell. Published by Macfarlane Walter & Ross, Toronto, 1994.

p. 122   "Inventor"
                Reprinted with permission of The Learning Partnership.

pp. 122-123   "The YMCA's Black Achievers"
                Reprinted with permission — The Toronto Star Syndicate.

pp. 124-125   "Mentors by Mail"
                Huron County Board of Education Website: huroned.edu.on.ca

pp. 141, 150   "The Know-Want-Learn Chart" and "My Response to Volunteering"
                Reprinted with permission from *Ages 12 Through 15: The Years of Transition* published by the Ontario Public School Teachers' Federation.

p. 153   "Employers Top Ten" (left portion only)
                Alberta Advanced Education & Career Development

p. 157–158   "Employability Skills Profile"
                Reprinted by permission of the Corporate Council on Education, a program of the National Business and Education Centre, The Conference Board of Canada

p. 160   "Pure Excitement"
                Reprinted with permission from *Career Paths* 1996, published by YES Canada — BC and funded by Human Resources Development Canada and the BC Ministry of Education, Skills and Training. For more information, Phone: (604) 435-1937, FAX: (604) 435-5548, E-mail: editor@careerpathsonline.com, Website: http://careerpathsonline.com

p. 175   "Describing Expectations"
                Reprinted with permission from *Ages 12 Through 15: The Years of Transition* published by the Ontario Public School Teachers' Federation.

pp. 180-181   "Building Your Work Skills in School"
                Adapted from Canada Career Information Partnership and *Canada Prospects*, 1996-97.

p. 189   "Serious Safety"
                Reprinted with permission from *Career Paths* 1996, published by YES Canada — BC and funded by Human Resources Development Canada and the BC Ministry of Education, Skills and Training. For more information, Phone: (604) 435-1937, FAX: (604) 435-5548, E-mail: editor@careerpathsonline.com, Website: http://careerpathsonline.com

Glossary

Action Plans   Steps to take to achieve goals.

Alternative Education Programs   Education programs that differ from traditional schooling, such as enrichment programs, flexible scheduling, and/or schools without formal classes.

Apprentice   A person being trained on-the-job by a qualified supervisor.

Aptitudes   Natural talents and abilities.

Attitudes   How a person views things.

Auditory Learners   People who learn best by listening.

Autobiography   The story of a person's life, told by that person.

Break Even   When a person's income (money earned) equals his or her expenses.

Budgeting   Planning what to do with money.

Business Plan   The way to keep track of the costs of starting up and running a business.

Career   A way of making a living, usually in a particular field of work. Can be categorized in four main areas, or clusters, namely Communication and the Arts; Engineering, Industrial, and Scientific Technology; Health, Human, and Public Services; and Business and Marketing.

Certification   A certificate proving that a person has achieved a course of study or a qualification.

Character References   Names and phone numbers of people who know a person well or with whom he or she has worked who can confirm the information given in a résumé or fact sheet.

Characteristics   Special qualities or features.

Cluster   Group.

Co-operative Education   An education program that offers, or combines, work experience with regular classes.

Collect, Select, Reflect Model   Refers to a Career Exploration Portfolio. A student collects items, selects pieces from the collection for a final presentation portfolio, and then reflects on the selections made.

Communication   Exchanging information through talking, writing, and behaviour.

Community   A group of people living in the same place under the same laws.

Community Service   Students volunteer their help to the community. Sometimes needed in order to graduate.

Community Services   Organizations that add to the quality of people's lives by providing services that promote health and well-being.

Compound Interest   A percentage of money the bank pays a person for letting them use, or invest, that person's money. It grows, or compounds, monthly.

Consult   To ask for an opinion.

Correspond   To communicate through writing letters.

Correspondence Courses   Study materials for courses are mailed to a student's home, where he or she completes them and mails them back for evaluation.

Creative Visualization   A method of focussed daydreaming, picturing something positive in one's mind.

Credits   When a student completes a course at high school, he or she receives a credit for it. A certain number of credits are required to earn a diploma.

Degree   What a student receives when he or she graduates from university.

Demographer   A person who studies the population of a country and determines what the future needs and what the actions of the population will be.

Diploma   The certificate a student receives when he or she graduates from high school or college.

Distance Education   Studying at home, using computer connections or long distance telephone calls to communicate with an instructor. For people who live far from available schools or universities.

Economy   The management of material resources.

Emotional Quotient (EQ)   The ability to handle one's emotions.

Entrepreneur   A person who recognizes a business opportunity and assumes the risk to make it into a business.

Expenses   The costs involved in running a business; what the business owner has to pay.

Fact Sheet   A brief list of information about a person to give to a possible employer or volunteer co-ordinator.

Futurist   A person who specializes in watching what is happening currently, observing changes, and predicting what will happen in the future.

Goals   Where a person wants to get to, or what a person wants to achieve.

Hourly Wage   The amount of money paid for working one hour. If a person works four hours, he or she receives that amount times four.

Human Rights   People's entitlement to fair treatment and justice.

Income   The amount of money a person earns.

Independent Learning Courses   Study materials for courses are mailed to a student's home, where he or she completes them and mails them back for evaluation.

Initiative   Doing something without being told to do it.

Intelligence Quotient (IQ)   A number that describes a person's intelligence, based on a standard test.

Interest Rate   The percentage per year of the amount of money borrowed.

International   Among nations; accepted by or agreed on by many or all nations, for the use of all nations.

Invest   Use money to buy something that is expected to make more money.

Job Shadowing   Spending a period of time at work with a person in a particular career, at a particular job.